COUNTRY *Afghans*

The Vanessa-Ann Collection

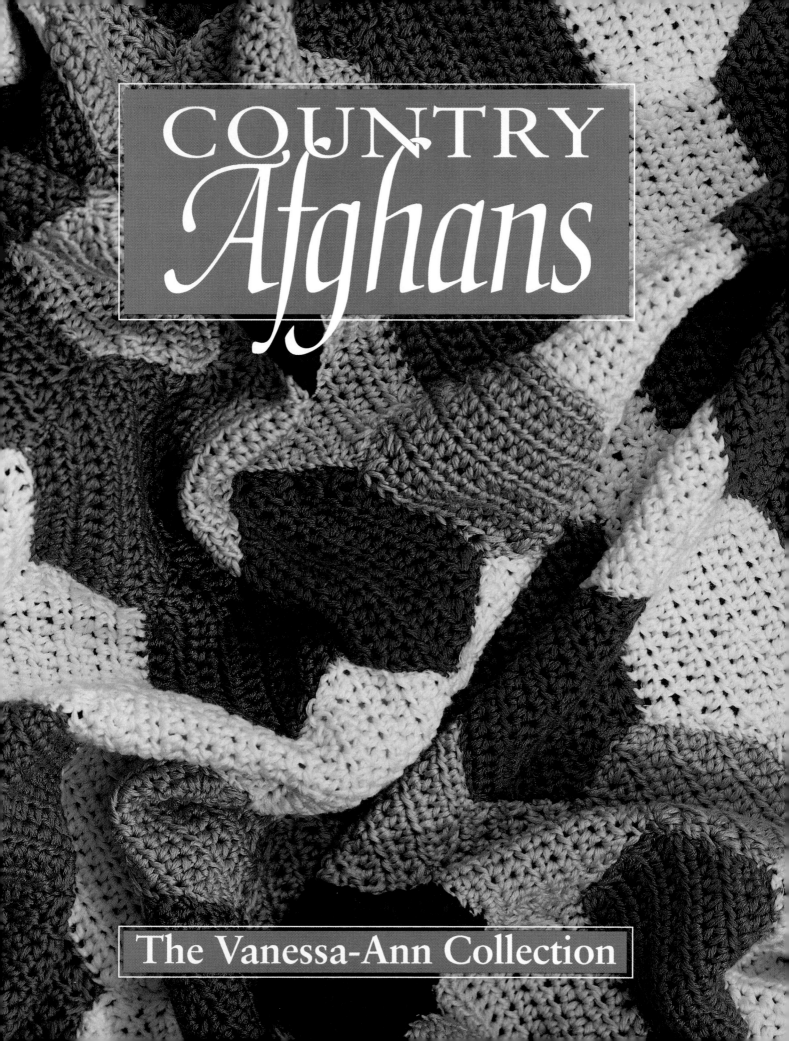

COUNTRY Afghans

The Vanessa-Ann Collection

For the Vanessa-Ann Collection
Owner: Jo Packham
Designers: Carrie Allen, Terrece Beesley, Trice Boerens,
    Marlene Lund, Jo Packham
Staff: Cherie Hanson, Tonya Jenkins, Susan Jorgensen,
    Margaret Shields Marti, Jackie McCowen, Barbara
    Milburn, Pamela Randall, Florence Stacey,
    Nancy Whitley

Photographer: Ryne Hazen

*The Vanessa-Ann Collection appreciates the trust and
cooperation of the individuals and businesses listed below
for allowing us to photograph on their premises and to
enjoy their treasures:*
    The Black Goose, Midvale, UT
    Penelope Hammons, Salt Lake City, UT
    Trends and Traditions, Ogden, UT
    RC Willey, Salt Lake City and Syracuse, UT
    Anita Louise, The Bearlace Cottage, Park City, UT
    Edie Stockstill, Salt Lake City, UT
    Jo Packham, Ogden, UT
    Madson's Furniture, Salt Lake City, UT

Country Afghans
from the *Crochet Treasury* Series

Library of Congress Catalog Card Number: 94-65422
Hardcover ISBN: 0-8487-1131-9
Softcover ISBN: 0-8487-1418-0
Manufactured in the United States of America
First Printing 1994

Editor-in-Chief: Nancy J. Fitzpatrick
Senior Crafts Editor: Susan Ramey Wright
Senior Editor, Editorial Services: Olivia Kindig Wells
Art Director: James Boone

Country Afghans

Editor: Margaret Allen Northen
Editorial Assistant: Rhonda Richards Wamble
Copy Editor: Susan Smith Cheatham
Designer: Elizabeth Passey Edge
Patterns and Illustrations: Melinda Johannson
Senior Production Designer: Larry Hunter
Publishing Systems Administrator: Rick Tucker
Production Manager: Rick Litton
Associate Production Manager: Theresa L. Beste
Production Assistant: Marianne Jordan
Additional Photography: Gary Clark, Mary-Gray Hunter

Contents

Cover Photo: Grandmother's Flowers, page 44.

Page 40

Page 54

Page 84

Page 130

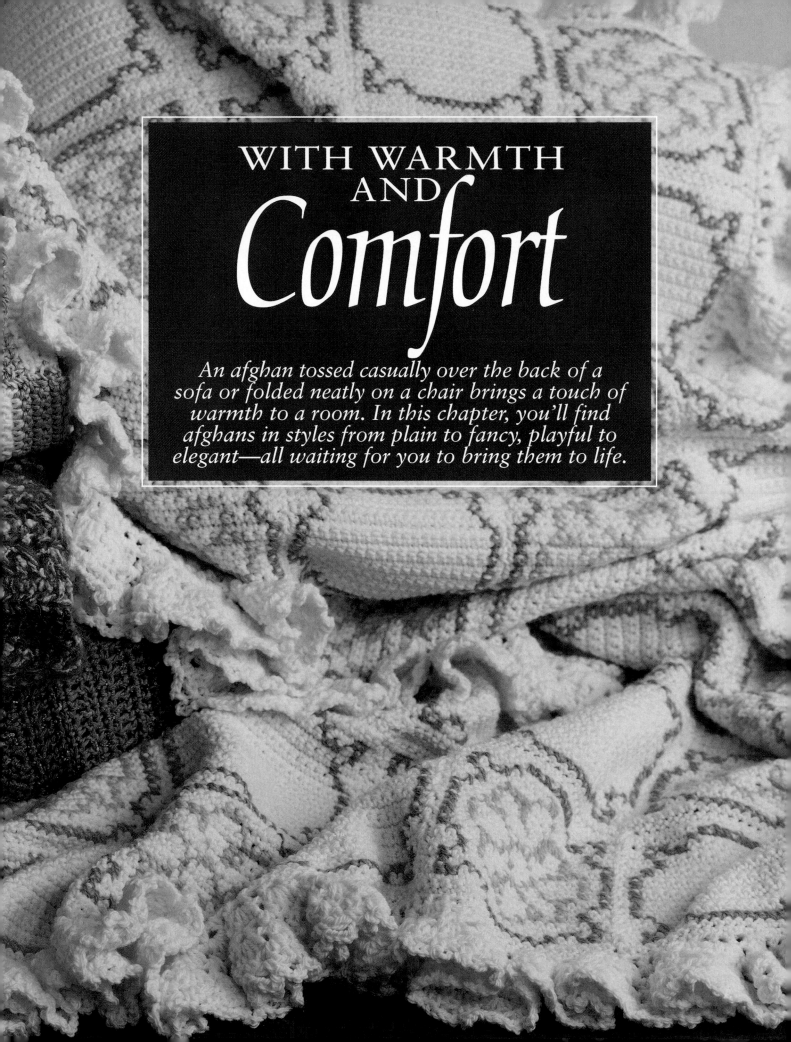

WITH WARMTH AND
Comfort

An afghan tossed casually over the back of a sofa or folded neatly on a chair brings a touch of warmth to a room. In this chapter, you'll find afghans in styles from plain to fancy, playful to elegant—all waiting for you to bring them to life.

Mosaic Medallions

*In this luscious afghan, a frilly
crocheted ruffle accents delicate
cross-stitched squares.*

FINISHED SIZE

Approximately 45" x 67", not including ruffle.

MATERIALS

Worsted-weight acrylic (110-yd. skein):
31 white.

Size G crochet hook, or size to obtain gauge.

Paternayan Persian wool (8-yd. skein): see color key.

GAUGE

4 sc and 5 rows = 1".

DIRECTIONS

Block (make 117): **Row 1:** With white, ch 22, sc in 2nd ch from hook and ea ch across = 21 sc, turn.

Rows 2–24: Ch 1, sc in ea st across, turn. Fasten off after row 24.

Cross-stitch: Centering design on block and using 2 strands of wool, cross-stitch complete design on 59 blocks. Centering design on block and using 2 strands of wool, cross-stitch blue border only on remaining 58 blocks.

Assembly: Afghan is 9 blocks wide and 13 blocks long. With right sides facing, whipstitch blocks together in a checkerboard pattern.

Ruffle: **Rnd 1:** With right side facing, join white with sl st in corner, ch 2 for sc and ch 1, sc in same st, * sc in ea st to last st of block, pull up a lp in last st of same block, pull up a lp in first st of next block, yo and pull through all lps on hook (sc dec over 2 sts made), rep from * across to corner of afghan, (sc, ch 1, sc) in corner, rep from * around, end with sl st in first ch of beg ch-2.

Rnd 2: Sl st into corner sp, ch 3 for first dc, (dc, ch 1, 2 dc) in same sp, * (ch 1, sk next st, dc in ea of next 2 sts) across to corner sp, ch 1, (2 dc, ch 1, 2 dc) in corner sp, rep from * around, end with sl st in top of beg ch-3 = 198 dc across ea long edge and 126 dc across ea short edge (not including corner grps).

Rnd 3: Sl st into corner sp, ch 3 for first dc, (dc, ch 1, 2 dc) in same sp, sk 2 dc and ch-1 sp, * [work 5 dc bet next 2 dc (5-dc shell made), sk 1 dc and ch-1 sp] across to corner sp, (2 dc, ch 1, 2 dc) in corner sp, rep from * around, end with sl st in top of beg ch-3.

Rnd 4: Sl st into corner sp, ch 3 for first dc, (dc, ch 1, 2 dc) in same sp, * ch 1, 2 dc in sp before next shell, (ch 1, 2 dc in center dc of next shell, ch 1, 2 dc in sp before next shell) across to corner sp, ch 1, (2 dc, ch 1, 2 dc) in corner sp, rep from * around, end with sl st in top of beg ch-3.

Rnd 5: Sl st into corner sp, ch 3 for first dc, (dc, ch 1, 2 dc) in same sp, sk 2 dc and ch-1 sp, * (5-dc shell bet next 2 dc, sk ch-1 sp) across to corner sp, (2 dc, ch 1, 2 dc) in corner sp, rep from * around, end with sl st in top of beg ch-3.

Rnd 6: Sl st into corner sp, ch 3 for first dc, (dc, ch 1, 2 dc) in same sp, * ch 1, 2 dc in sp before next shell, (ch 1, sc in center dc of next shell, ch 1, 2 dc in sp before next shell) across to corner sp, ch 1, (2 dc, ch 1, 2 dc) in corner sp, rep from * around, end with sl st in top of beg ch-3.

Rnd 7: Sl st into corner sp, ch 6 for sc and ch 5, sc in same sp, * (ch 5, sc in next ch-1 sp) across to corner sp, ch 5, (sc, ch 5, sc) in corner sp, rep from * around, end with sl st in first ch of beg ch-6. Fasten off.

Cross-stitch Chart

Nursery Rhymes

Textured blocks in soft pastel colors make this coverlet perfect for your favorite little one.

FINISHED SIZE
Approximately 40" x 57".

MATERIALS
Worsted-weight cotton (109-yd. ball): 3 each white, light yellow; 4 each baby pink, mint green, baby blue, aqua, light purple.

Size F crochet hook, or size to obtain gauge.

GAUGE
4 dc = 1".

DIRECTIONS
Shell block (make 5 baby pink; 4 ea white, light yellow, mint green, baby blue, aqua, purple): **Row 1** (wrong side): Ch 27, (sc, hdc, dc) in 3rd ch from hook, * sk next 2 ch, (sc, hdc, dc) in next ch, rep from * 6 times more, sk 2 ch, sc in last ch, turn.

Row 2: Ch 1, (hdc, dc) in same st, * (sc, hdc, dc) in next sc, rep from * 6 times more, sc in last st, turn.

Rows 3–18: Rep row 2. Fasten off after row 18.

Dc block (make 3 ea baby pink, light yellow, mint green, baby blue, aqua, purple; 1 white): **Row 1** (right side): Ch 27, dc in 4th ch from hook and ea ch across, turn = 25 sts.

Row 2: Ch 1, working in ft lps only, ch 1, sc in ea st across, turn.

Row 3: Ch 3 for first dc, working through both lps, dc in ea st across, turn.

Rows 4–15: Rep rows 2 and 3 alternately. Fasten off after row 15.

Assembly: Afghan is 6 blocks wide and 8 blocks long. With right sides facing, whipstitch blocks together as desired.

Edging: **Rnd 1:** *Note:* To work across long edge of afghan, work 2 sts in side of ea dc row and 1 st in side of ea sc row. With right side facing, join baby pink with sl st in any corner, ch 3 for first dc, * (dc in ea of next 2 sts, ch 3, sk next 3 sts, dc in ea of next 3 sts) across to corner, (dc, ch 3, dc) in corner, rep from * around, end with sl st in top of beg ch-3. Fasten off.

Rnd 2: Working over and around corner ch-3 lp, join purple with sl st in corner of afghan, ch 3 for first dc, 2 dc in same corner, * (ch 3, sk next 3 dc of rnd 1, working over and around ch-3 lp of rnd 1, dc in ea of 3 unworked sts on edge of afghan) across to corner, ch 3, working over and around corner ch-3 lp, (3 dc, ch 3, 3 dc) in corner of afghan, rep from * around, end with sl st in top of beg ch-3. Fasten off.

Rnd 3: Join mint green with sl st in any corner lp, ch 1, sc in same lp, * (ch 3, sk next 3 dc, working over and around ch-3 lp of rnd 2, dc in ea of next 3 rnd-1 dc sts) across to corner, ch 3, (2 sc, ch 1, 2 sc) in corner lp, rep from * around, end with sl st in top of beg ch-1. Fasten off.

Rnd 4: Join aqua in corner ch-1 sp, ch 1, * sc in ea of next 2 sc, (working over and around ch-3 lp of rnd 3, dc in ea of next 3 rnd-2 dc sts, ch 3, sk next 3 dc) across to corner, sc in ea of next 2 sc, sc in corner ch-1 sp, rep from * around, end with sl st in beg ch-1. Fasten off.

Rnd 5: Join baby blue with sl st in center st of any corner, ch 2 for first hdc, * hdc in ea of next 2 sc, (sc in ea of next 3 dc, working over and around ch-3 lp of rnd 4, dc in ea of next 3 rnd-3 dc sts) across to 3 dc before corner, sc in ea of next 3 dc, hdc in ea of next 2 sc, (hdc, ch 1, hdc) in center corner st, rep from * around, end with sl st in top of beg ch-2. Fasten off.

Ruffled Yo-Yos

To make this doll-sized throw, accent crocheted yo-yo rounds with touches of candy-colored thread.

FINISHED SIZE
Approximately 23" x 33".

MATERIALS
Size 5 crochet cotton (218-yd. ball): 17 white; 1 each medium mint, medium rose, medium purple.
Size 2 steel crochet hook, or size to obtain gauge.

GAUGE
Yo-yo = 2¼" diameter.

DIRECTIONS
Yo-yo (make 156): With white, ch 6, join with a sl st to form a ring.

Rnd 1: Ch 3 for first dc, 17 dc in ring, sl st in top of beg ch-3.

Rnd 2: Ch 3 for first dc, dc in same st, (dc in next dc, 2 dc in next dc) 8 times, dc in next dc, sl st in top of beg ch-3.

Rnd 3: Ch 3 for first dc, dc in same st, (dc in next dc, 2 dc in next dc) 13 times, sl st in top of beg ch-3.

Rnd 4: Ch 1, sc in same st and ea st around, sl st in first sc.

Rnd 5: Ch 3 for first dc, dc in same st, 2 dc in ea st around, sl st in top of beg ch-3.

Rnd 6: Ch 3 for first dc, dc in ea st around, sl st in top of beg ch-3.

Rnd 7: Ch 1, sc in ea st around, sl st in first sc. Fasten off.

Ruffle (make 50 medium mint, 52 medium purple, 54 medium rose): Join thread in any rnd-7 sc of yo-yo, (ch 5, sk next sc, sc in next sc) around, end with ch 5, sl st in first ch of beg ch-5. Fasten off, leaving a tail of thread. *To gather yo-yo:* weave tail of thread * over 1 rnd-7 sc and under next 7 sc sts, rep from * around. Pull up tightly and secure thread.

Assembly: For each whole flower, arrange 6 outer yo-yos in a circle around center yo-yo and tack together. Make the number shown in parentheses, arranging colors as specified.

Whole flower	Center yo-yo	6 outer yo-yos
A (3)	Medium rose	Medium mint
B (2)	Medium rose	Medium purple
C (3)	Medium mint	Medium rose
D (4)	Medium mint	Medium purple
E (3)	Medium purple	Medium rose
F (3)	Medium purple	Medium mint

For each half flower, arrange 4 outer yo-yos in a half circle around center yo-yo and tack together. Make the number shown in parentheses, arranging colors as specified.

Half flower	Center yo-yo	4 outer yo-yos
G (1)	Medium rose	Medium purple
H (2)	Medium mint	Medium rose
I (1)	Medium mint	Medium purple
J (1)	Medium purple	Medium rose
K (1)	Medium purple	Medium mint

Finishing: Referring to placement diagram, tack whole and half flowers together.

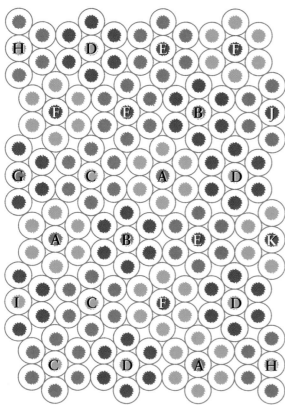

Placement Diagram

Buttoned-Down

Wooden buttons add interesting texture to this afghan stitched with a nubby, variegated yarn.

FINISHED SIZE
Approximately 40" x 42".

MATERIALS
Worsted-weight cotton-mohair-acrylic blend bouclé (66-yd. skein): 5 variegated mauve/green/ecru.

Worsted-weight wool-mohair-acrylic blend (146-yd. skein): 5 dark rose, 1 turquoise.

Size G crochet hook, or size to obtain gauge.

42 (1") buttons.

GAUGE
Square = 4".

DIRECTIONS
Square (make 56): **Row 1:** With variegated yarn, ch 13, hdc in 3rd ch from hook and ea ch across, turn = 12 hdc.

Row 2: Ch 3 for first dc, * sk next st, dc in next st, working backward in front of prev dc, dc in sk st (cross st made), rep from * 4 times more, dc in last st, turn = 5 cross sts.

Row 3: Ch 2 for first hdc, hdc in ea st across, turn.

Rows 4–7: Rep rows 2 and 3, alternately. Fasten off after row 7.

Border: Join dark rose with sl st in any corner, ch 1, * sc in ea st to next corner, 3 sc in corner, rep from * around, end with sl st in beg ch-1. Fasten off.

Assembly: Center panel is 7 squares wide and 8 squares long. With right sides facing, whipstitch squares together. Stitch 1 button in place at each intersection of 4 squares (see photo).

End panel: **Row 1:** With wrong side of center panel facing, join dark rose with sl st in top right-hand corner, ch 2 for first hdc, work 13 hdc across ea square to last square before corner, work 14 hdc across last square, turn = 93 sts.

Row 2: Ch 2 for first hdc, hdc in ea of next 5 sts, * ch 1, (yo and pull up a lp) twice in ea of next 3 sts, yo and pull through all lps on hook (cl over 3 sts made), ch 1, hdc in ea of next 10 sts, rep from * across, end last rep with hdc in ea of last 6 sts, turn.

Row 3: Ch 2 for first hdc, hdc in ea st across, turn.

Row 4: Ch 3 for first dc, (cross st over next 2 sts) 45 times, hdc in ea of last 2 sts, turn.

Row 5: Rep row 3.

Row 6: Ch 2 for first hdc, hdc in ea of next 11 sts, * ch 1, cl over next 3 sts, ch 1, hdc in ea of next 10 sts, rep from * across to last 3 sts, hdc in ea of last 3 sts, turn.

Rows 7 and 8: Rep rows 3 and 4.

Row 9: Rep row 3.

Rows 10 and 11: Rep rows 2 and 3. Fasten off after row 11.

Rep to work end panel on opposite edge of center panel.

Side panel: **Row 1:** With wrong side facing and center panel turned to work across side edge, join dark rose with sl st in corner st of center panel, ch 2 for first hdc, rep row 1 as for end panel, turn = 106 sts.

Rows 2–11: Rep rows 2–11 as for end panel. Fasten off after row 11.

Rep to work side panel on rem edge of center panel.

Corner block (make 4): **Row 1** (wrong side): With turquoise, ch 21, hdc in 3rd ch from hook and ea ch across, turn = 20 sts.

Row 2: Ch 2 for first hdc, hdc in next st, ch 1, * cl over next 3 sts, ch 1, hdc in ea of next 10 sts, ch 1, cl over next 3 sts, ch 1, hdc in ea of last 2 sts, turn.

Row 3: Ch 2 for first hdc, hdc in ea st across, turn = 20 sts.

Row 4: Ch 3 for first dc, (cross st over next 2 sts) 9 times, dc in last st, turn.

Row 5: Rep row 3.

Row 6: Ch 2 for first hdc, hdc in ea of next 7 sts, ch 1, cl over next 3 sts, ch 1, hdc in ea of last 9 sts, turn.

Rows 7 and 8: Rep rows 3 and 4.

Row 9: Rep row 3.

Rows 10 and 11: Rep rows 2 and 3. Fasten off after row 11.

Assembly: With right sides facing, whipstitch corner blocks to afghan.

Edging: **Rnd 1:** With right side facing, join dark rose with sl st in any corner, ch 1, * sc in ea st to corner, dec as necessary to keep work flat, (sc, ch 1, sc) in corner, rep from * around, end with sl st in beg ch-1.

Rnd 2: Ch 1, * sc in ea st to corner, (sc, ch 1, sc) in corner sp, rep from * around, end with sl st in beg ch-1. Fasten off.

Count to Nine

Easy squares made in shades of blue and green join to create the nine-patch blocks in this coverlet.

FINISHED SIZE
Approximately 48" x 60".

MATERIALS
Sportweight cotton-polyester blend (106-yd. ball): 2 medium country blue; 4 each light country green, medium country green, medium aqua; 9 medium country purple.
Size F crochet hook, or size to obtain gauge.

GAUGE
8 sc and 9 rows = 2".

DIRECTIONS
Square (make 17 medium country blue, 28 light country green, 30 medium country green, 33 medium aqua): **Row 1:** Ch 13, sc in 2nd ch from hook and ea ch across, turn = 13 sc.
 Rows 2–13: Ch 1, sc in ea st across, turn. Fasten off after row 13.

Triangle (make 48): **Row 1:** With medium country purple, ch 2, sc in 2nd ch from hook, turn.
 Row 2: Ch 2, sc in 2nd ch from hook, 2 sc in next st, turn.
 Row 3: Ch 2, sc in 2nd ch from hook, sc in ea of next 2 sts, 2 sc in next st, leave last st unworked, turn.
 Rows 4–19: Ch 2, sc in 2nd ch from hook, sc in ea st across to last 2 sts, 2 sc in next st, leave last st unworked, turn. Fasten off after row 19.

Assembly: With right sides facing, whipstitch squares together as desired to form 9-patch blocks. Whipstitch 1 triangle to each edge of each 9-patch block. Afghan is 3 blocks wide and 4 blocks long. With right sides facing and 9-patch blocks turned on point, whipstitch blocks together (see photo).

Edging: **Rnd 1:** With right side facing, join medium country purple with sl st in corner, ch 2 for sc and ch 1, sc in same st, * sc across to next corner, (sc, ch 1, sc) in corner, rep from * around, end with sl st in first ch of beg ch-2, sl st into corner sp, turn.
 Rnd 2: Ch 2 for sc and ch 1, sc in same corner sp, * sc in ea st to corner sp, (sc, ch 1, sc) in corner sp, rep from * around, end with sl st in first ch of beg ch-2, sl st into corner sp, turn.
 Rnd 3: Ch 4 for first dc and ch 1, dc in same corner sp, * dc in ea st to corner sp, (dc, ch 1, dc) in corner sp, rep from * around, end with sl st in 3rd ch of beg ch-4, sl st into corner sp, turn.
 Rnd 4: Rep rnd 2. Fasten off.
 Rnd 5: With right side facing, join medium aqua with sl st in any corner sp, rep rnd 2.
 Rnd 6: Ch 4 for first dc and ch 1, 2 dc in same corner sp, * dc in ea st to corner sp, (2 dc, ch 1, 2 dc) in corner sp, rep from * around, end with dc in beg corner, sl st in 3rd ch of beg ch-4, sl st into corner sp, turn.
 Rnds 7 and 8: Rep rnd 2.
 Rnd 9: Rep rnd 6.
 Rnd 10: Rep rnd 2. Fasten off.
 Rnd 11: With right side facing, join medium country purple with sl st in any corner sp, rep rnd 2.
 Rnd 12: Rep rnd 6. Fasten off.
 Rnd 13: With right side facing, join medium country blue with sl st in any corner sp, rep rnd 2.
 Rnd 14: Rep rnd 2.
 Rnd 15: Rep rnd 6.
 Rnd 16: Rep rnd 2. Fasten off.
 Rnd 17: With right side facing, join medium country purple with sl st in any corner sp, rep rnd 2. Do not turn.
 Rnd 18: Working in crab st (reverse sc) from left to right (instead of right to left), sc around afghan (sk sts as necessary to keep work flat), end with sl st in first sc. Fasten off.

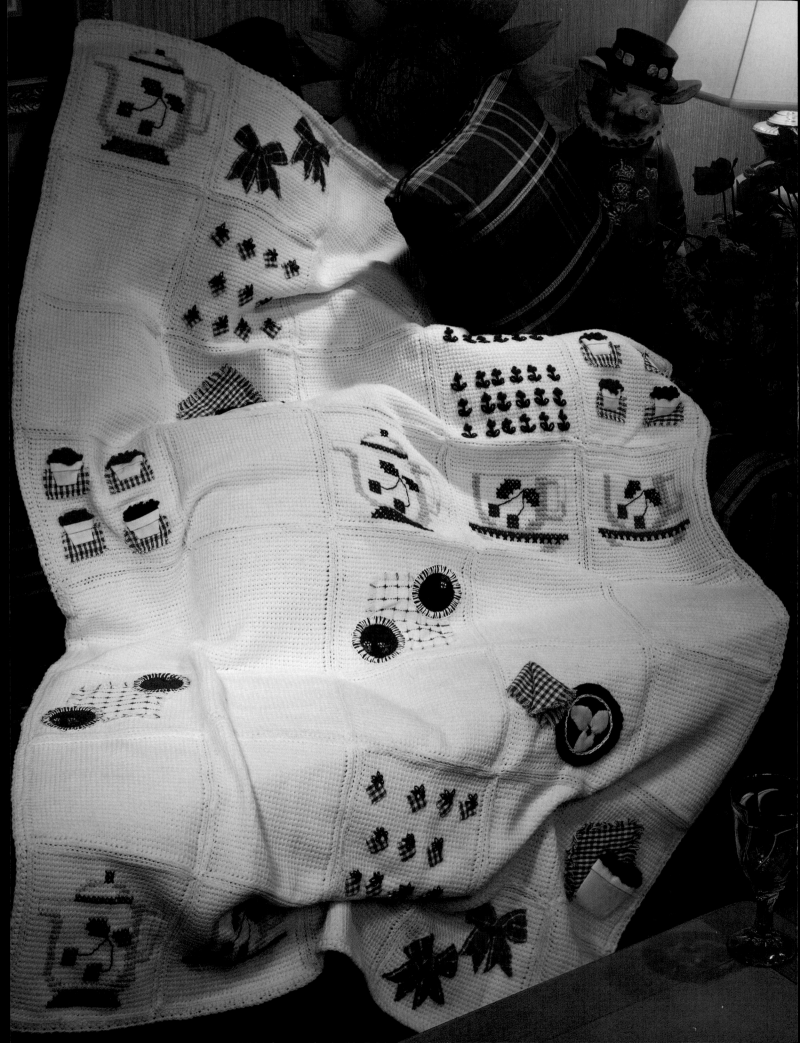

Teatime

*Cross-stitch, appliqué, and embroider a plain
white afghan with a medley of teapots,
teacups, fruits and flowers, and fancy bows.*

FINISHED SIZE
Approximately 45" x 69".

MATERIALS
Sportweight acrylic (175-yd. skein): 15 white.
Size I afghan hook, or size to obtain gauge.
Sizes F and G crochet hooks.
Paternayan Persian wool (8-yd. skein): see color key, plus 4 Green #680; 6 each Navy #571, Dark Red #969.
Size 5 pearl cotton (53-yd. ball): 2 each White, Emerald Green #909.
Cotton fabrics: 6" x 14" piece of red-and-white stripe, 9" square of navy, 6" x 7" piece of yellow, 10" x 12" square of red-and-white check, 5" x 9" piece of blue-and-white stripe, 8" x 12" piece of green-and-white check, 10" x 12" piece of white fabric.
Sewing thread to match fabrics.

GAUGE
4 sts and 4 rows = 1" in afghan st.

DIRECTIONS
Note: See page 141 for afghan st directions.

Block (make 40): With white and afghan hook, ch 36, work 30 rows afghan st. Sl st in ea vertical bar across. Do not fasten off.
Border: With size G hook, ch 1, * sc in ea st to next corner, (sc, ch 1, sc) in corner, rep from * around, end with sl st in beg ch-1. Fasten off.

Finishing: Teapot block (make 3): Using 2 strands of Persian wool, cross-stitch 1 teapot on each of 3 blocks according to chart. Use 1 strand of light blue Persian wool for backstitching.
Teacup block (make 3): Using 2 strands of Persian wool, cross-stitch 1 teacup on each of 3 blocks according to chart. Use 1 strand of light blue Persian wool for backstitching.
Flowers block (make 1): Beginning 2 rows from bottom edge and 5 stitches from left edge of crocheted block, stitch rows of flowers on block as follows. Referring to photo and using 3 strands of green Persian wool, make 2 lazy daisy stitches for leaves; straightstitch stem. Using 3 strands of dark

red Persian wool, make 3 French knots at top of stem for flower. Repeat to stitch rows of flowers on block as desired.
Bows block (make 2): Cut 4 (1½" x 14") strips of red-and-white stripe fabric. Tie each strip in a bow. Stitch 2 bows to each of 2 blocks.
Lemons block (make 2): For each block, cut 1 (4¼"-diameter) circle from navy fabric and 3 lemons from yellow fabric, adding ⅛" seam allowance to pattern. Appliqué lemons to navy circle. Satin-stitch leaves on lemons using 3 strands of green Persian wool. Baste navy circle to crocheted block (see photo). Using 2 strands of navy Perisan wool, work ⅝" buttonhole stitch around edge of circle. Using 2 strands of white size 5 pearl cotton, work a chainstitch circle on navy fabric inside buttonhole stitching. For napkin, cut 1 (6") square of red-and-white check fabric and fringe edges. Fold square into quarters and tack point of fold to block (see photo).
Strawberries block (make 2): For each block, cut 11 (1½") squares of red-and-white check fabric. Fold under ¼" around edge of each square and press. Arrange squares on point in 3 rows and stitch to crocheted block (see photo). For leaves, using 3 strands of emerald green size 5 pearl cotton, make 6 lazy daisy stitches at top of each strawberry.
Strawberry picnic block (make 2): For each block, cut 1 (4½") square of blue-and-white stripe fabric. Fringe edges. Stitch fabric to crocheted block. Cut 2 (3"-diameter) circles from navy fabric. Arrange circles on block, overlapping blue-and-white fabric (see photo). Using 2 strands of white size 5 pearl cotton, work ½" buttonhole stitch around edge of each circle. For each strawberry, satin-stitch berry on plate using 3 strands of dark red Persian wool. Make French knots for seeds with 1 strand of white size 5 pearl cotton. For leaves, using 4 strands of emerald green size 5 pearl cotton, make 3 lazy daisy stitches. Repeat to stitch additional strawberries on plates as desired.
Blueberries block (make 2): For each block, cut 1 (5") square of green-and-white check fabric. Fringe edges. Arrange square on point on crocheted block and stitch. Cut 1 large carton from white fabric, adding ¼" seam allowance to side

19

and bottom edges. Fold top edge of carton to right side twice as indicated on pattern and press. Fold under ¼" on side and bottom edges and press. Slipstitch carton to crocheted block, overlapping green-and-white fabric (see photo). For blueberries, using 3 strands of navy Persian wool, make several rows of French knots along top edge of carton.

Berry cartons block (make 2): For each block, cut 4 (1½" x 2½") pieces of green-and-white check fabric. Fringe edges of each piece. Cut 4 small cartons from white fabric, adding ¼" seam allowance to side and bottom edges. Fold top edge of each carton to right side twice as indicated on pattern and press. Fold under ¼" on side and bottom edges and press. Position green-and-white check pieces and small cartons on crocheted block as shown in photo and stitch. Using 3 strands of navy (for blueberries) or dark red (for raspberries)

Persian wool, make several rows of French knots along top edge of each carton.

Assembly: Afghan is 5 blocks wide and 8 blocks long. With right sides facing and working through back loops only, whipstitch blocks together as desired.

Edging: **Rnd 1:** With wrong side facing and size F hook, join white with sl st in any corner, ch 1, working in ft lps only, * sc in ea st to corner, (sc, ch 1, sc) in corner, rep from * around, end with sl st in beg ch-1, turn.

Rnd 2: With size G hook, sl st into corner sp, ch 2 for sc and ch 1, * (sk next st, sc in next st, ch 1) across to corner sp, (sc, ch 1, sc) in corner sp, ch 1, rep from * around, end with sl st in first ch of beg ch-2. Fasten off.

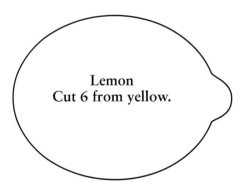

Lemon
Cut 6 from yellow.

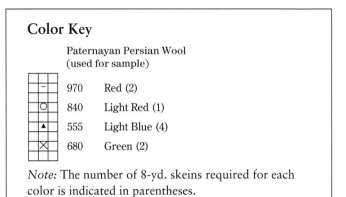

Color Key

Paternayan Persian Wool
(used for sample)

−	970	Red (2)
○	840	Light Red (1)
▲	555	Light Blue (4)
✕	680	Green (2)

Note: The number of 8-yd. skeins required for each color is indicated in parentheses.

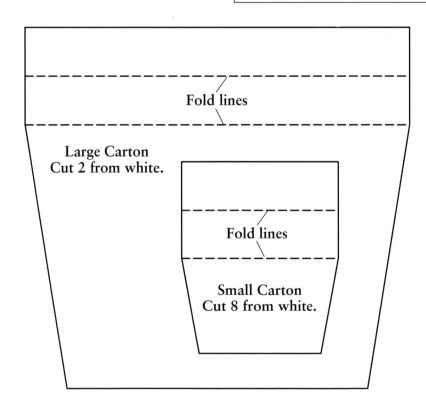

Fold lines

Large Carton
Cut 2 from white.

Fold lines

Small Carton
Cut 8 from white.

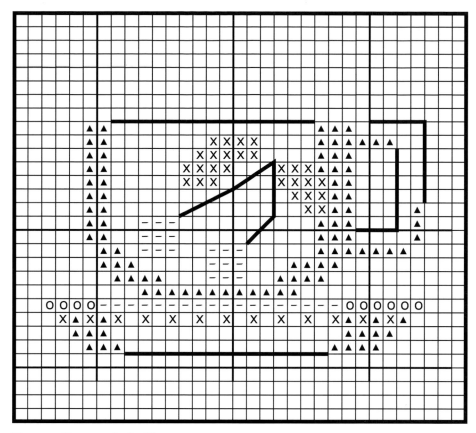

Teacup Cross-stitch Chart

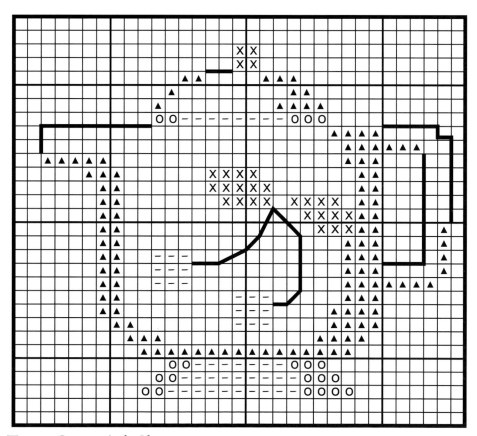

Teapot Cross-stitch Chart

Bright Blossoms

Vibrant puff-stitch flower motifs give this throw the look of a sun-washed flower bed.

FINISHED SIZE
Approximately 40" x 56".

MATERIALS
Sportweight acrylic (175-yd. ball): 1 each light yellow, bright red; 2 each hot pink, dark blue; 3 dark yellow; 4 red; 6 green.
Sportweight acrylic-wool blend (150-yd. ball): 2 violet.
Size E crochet hook, or size to obtain gauge.

GAUGE
Flower = 3½".
Square = 1½".

DIRECTIONS
Flower (make the number shown in parentheses using colors as foll):

Flower	Rnds 1–3	Rnds 4–6
A (30)	Light yellow	Hot pink
B (16)	Dark yellow	Bright red
C (48)	Dark yellow	Red
D (16)	Dark yellow	Dark blue
E (14)	Dark yellow	Violet
F (30)	Green	Green

Rnd 1: With first color, ch 2, 7 sc in 2nd ch from hook, sl st in top of beg ch-2 = 8 sts.

Rnd 2: Ch 1, sc in same st, (yo and pull up a lp) 5 times in next st, yo and pull through all lps on hook (puff made), ch 3, puff in same st, * ch 1, sc in next st, (puff, ch 3, puff) in next st, rep from * twice more, ch 1, sl st in first sc.

Rnd 3: Ch 1, sc in same st, * sc in next puff, sc in next ch, (sc, ch 1, sc) in next ch for corner, sc in next ch, sc in next puff, sc in next sc, rep from * around, end with sl st in first sc. Fasten off.

Rnd 4: Join next color with sl st in any corner sp, ch 1, sc in same sp, * sc in next st, hdc in next st, dc in next st, 3 tr in next st, dc in next st, hdc in next st, sc in next st, sc in next corner sp, rep from * around, end with sl st in first sc.

Rnd 5: Ch 3 for first dc, sk 1 sc, * dc in next hdc, 3 dc in next dc, dc in ea of next 3 tr, 3 dc in next dc, dc in next hdc, sk 1 sc, dc in next sc, sk 1 sc, rep from * around, end with sl st in top of beg ch-3.

Rnd 6: Ch 1, sc in ea of next 2 sts, * (sc, ch 1, sc) in next st, sc in ea of next 5 sts, rep from * around, end with sl st in beg ch-1. Fasten off.

Square (make 149): **Row 1:** With green, ch 7, sc in 2nd ch from hook and ea ch across, turn.

Rows 2–7: Ch 1, sc in ea st across, turn = 7 sts. Fasten off after row 7.

Assembly: Arrange colored flowers as desired, alternating with green squares and using green flowers around outside edges (see photo). With right sides facing, whipstitch motifs together.

Checkmate

Wrap your loved ones in a throw of bright
red-and-white squares dotted with hearts.

Finished Size

Approximately 45" x 46".

Materials

Sportweight acrylic (175-yd. ball): 4 white, 8 red. Sizes F and G crochet hooks, or size to obtain gauge.

Gauge

5 hdc and 3 rows = 1" with size G hook.

Directions

Block (make 85 white, 84 red): **Row 1:** With size G hook, ch 13, hdc in 3rd ch from hook and ea ch across = 12 hdc.

Rows 2–7: Ch 2 for first hdc, * hdc in bk lp only of next st, hdc in ft lp only of next st, rep from * across, hdc in last st, turn. Fasten off after row 7.

Heart (make 9): **Rnd 1** (right side): With size F hook and red, ch 5, 2 dc in 4th ch from hook, (hdc, dc, hdc) in next ch, working in opposite side of base ch, 2 dc in same ch as beg, ch 3, sl st in same ch, turn.

Rnd 2: Ch 2, 2 hdc in top of next ch-3, hdc in ea of next 3 sts, (hdc, dc, hdc) in next st for point of heart, hdc in ea of next 3 sts, 2 hdc in top of next ch-3, ch 2, sl st in center of heart, turn.

Rnd 3: Ch 2, hdc in top of prev ch-2, 2 hdc in ea of next 2 sts, sc in ea of next 4 sts, (hdc, dc, hdc) in next st for point of heart, sc in ea of next 4 sts, 2 hdc in ea of next 2 sts, hdc in top of ch-2, ch 2, sl st in center of heart. Fasten off.

Assembly: Center panel of afghan is 13 blocks square. With right sides facing, whipstitch blocks together in a checkerboard pattern.

Whipstitch hearts to white afghan blocks as desired (see photo).

Edging: **Rnd 1:** With wrong side facing and using size G hook, join red with sl st in any corner, ch 3 for first hdc and ch 1, hdc in same st, (yo and pull up a lp) twice in same st, (yo and pull up a lp) twice in next st, yo and pull through all lps on hook, ch 1 (cl made), * sk 2 sts, hdc in next st, work first leg of cl in same st as prev hdc and 2nd leg in next st as est, rep from * across to corner, (hdc, ch 1, hdc) in corner, work first leg of cl in same st as prev st and 2nd leg in next st as est, rep from * around, end with sl st in 2nd ch of beg ch-3, sl st into ch-1 sp, turn = 39 cl across ea edge.

Rnd 2 (right side): Ch 3 for first hdc and ch 1, hdc in same corner sp, * hdc in ea st across to corner sp, (hdc, ch 1, hdc) in corner, rep from * around, end with sl st in 2nd ch of beg ch-3, sl st into corner sp, turn.

Rnds 3 and 4: Ch 3 for first hdc and ch 1, hdc in same corner sp, * (hdc in bk lp only of next st, hdc in ft lp only of next st) across to corner sp, (hdc, ch 1, hdc) in corner sp, rep from * around, end with sl st in 2nd ch of beg ch-3, sl st into corner sp, turn.

Rnd 5: Ch 3 for first hdc and ch 1, hdc in same corner sp, work first leg of cl in same sp and 2nd leg in next st, * (sk next st, hdc in next st, work first leg of cl in same st as prev st and 2nd leg in next st as est) across to 1 st before corner sp, hdc in next st, (hdc, ch 1, hdc) in corner sp, rep from * around, end with sl st in 2nd ch of beg ch-3, sl st into corner sp, turn.

Rnds 6–10: Rep rnds 2–5, ending after rnd 2. Fasten off after rnd 10.

Rnd 11: With wrong side facing, join white with sl st in any corner sp, ch 3 for first hdc and ch 1, hdc in same sp, * [hdc in ea of next 2 sts, yo and insert hook from back to front around post of next st, complete st as a dc (back post dc made), back post dc around post of next st] across to 3 sts before corner sp, hdc in ea of next 3 sts, (hdc, ch 1, hdc) in corner sp, rep from * around, end with sl st in 2nd ch of beg ch-3, turn. Fasten off.

Rnd 12: With right side facing, join red with sl st in any corner sp, ch 3 for first hdc and ch 1, hdc in same sp, * hdc in ea of next 2 sts, yo twice and insert hook from front to back around post of rnd-10 corner hdc, complete st as a tr (front post tr made), front post tr around next rnd-10 hdc, (sk 2 rnd-11 sts, hdc in ea of next 2 rnd-11 sts, front post tr around ea of next 2 rnd-10 hdc) across to 1 st before corner, hdc in next st, (hdc, ch 1, hdc) in corner sp, rep from * around, end with sl st in 2nd ch of beg ch-3, turn. Fasten off.

Rnd 13: With wrong side facing, join white with sl st in any corner sp, ch 3 for first hdc and ch 1, hdc in same sp, * hdc in ea of next 2 sts, (back post dc around ea of next 2 tr, hdc in ea of next 2 hdc) across to 1 st before corner, hdc in next st, (hdc, ch 1, hdc) in corner sp, rep from * around, end with sl st in 2nd ch of beg ch-3, turn. Fasten off.

Rnd 14: With right side facing, join red with sl st in any corner sp, ch 3 for first hdc and ch 1, hdc in same sp, hdc in ea of next 2 rnd-13 sts, * (front post tr around ea of next 2 rnd-12 hdc, hdc in ea of next 2 rnd-13 sts) to 1 st before corner, hdc in next st, (hdc, ch 1, hdc) in corner sp, rep from * around, end with sl st in 2nd ch of beg ch-3, sl st into corner sp, turn.

Rnd 15: Rep rnd 5.

Rnds 16–19: Rep rnds 2–5.

Rnd 20: With right side facing, ch 1, working in crab st (reverse sc) from left to right (instead of right to left), * sc in ea st to corner, (sc, ch 1, sc) in corner, rep from * around. Fasten off.

Plain Geometry

*Appliqué crocheted circles, squares, stars,
and triangles to a bright background
for this afghan with kids' appeal.*

FINISHED SIZE

Approximately 41" x 50".

MATERIALS

Sportweight acrylic-wool blend (150-yd. ball): 2 bright green.

Sportweight acrylic (175-yd. ball): 3 dark yellow; 2 each bright blue, hot pink; 1 bright red.

Size G crochet hook, or size to obtain gauge.

GAUGE

2 (2-dc cl) = 1".

6 pat rows = 2½".

Note: Each finished piece should measure the size given in the directions.

DIRECTIONS

Bright green strip 1 (3" x 30"): **Row 1** (wrong side): With bright green, ch 14, keeping last lp of ea dc on hook, dc in 4th ch from hook, sk next ch, dc in next ch, yo and pull through rem lps on hook (2-dc cl made), * ch 1, keeping last lp of ea dc on hook, dc in same ch as last leg of prev cl, sk next ch, dc in next ch, yo and pull through rem lps on hook (2-dc cl made), rep from * across, dc in same st as last leg of prev cl, turn.

Row 2 (right side): Ch 2, sc in next ch-1 sp, (ch 1, sc in next ch-1 sp) across, sc in top of tch, turn.

Row 3: Ch 3, work 2-dc cl over same st as tch and next sc, ch 1, * work 2-dc cl over same sc as last leg of prev cl and next sc, ch 1, rep from * across, dc in same st as last leg of prev cl, turn.

Rows 4–74: Rep rows 2 and 3 alternately, until piece measures 30" from beg. Fasten off after row 74.

Bright green strip 2 (2" x 40"): **Row 1:** With bright green, ch 10, rep row 1 as for bright green strip 1.

Rows 2–84: Rep rows 2 and 3 alternately as for bright green strip 1, until piece measures 40" from beg. Fasten off after row 84.

Hot pink panel (8" x 40"): **Row 1:** With hot pink, ch 34, rep row 1 as for bright green strip 1.

Rows 2–84: Rep rows 2 and 3 alternately as for bright green strip 1, until piece measures 40" from beg. Fasten off after row 84.

Hot pink block (10" square): **Row 1:** With hot pink, ch 44, rep row 1 as for bright green strip 1.

Rows 2–28: Rep rows 2 and 3 alternately as for bright green strip 1, until piece measures 10" from beg. Fasten off after row 28.

Bright blue panel (10" x 30"): **Row 1:** With bright blue, ch 44, rep row 1 as for bright green strip 1.

Rows 2–74: Rep rows 2 and 3 alternately as for bright green strip 1, until piece measures 30" from beg. Fasten off after row 74.

Dark yellow panel 1 (10" x 30"): **Row 1:** With dark yellow, ch 44, rep row 1 as for bright green strip 1.

Rows 2–74: Rep rows 2 and 3 alternately as for bright green strip 1, until piece measures 30" from beg. Fasten off after row 74.

Dark yellow panel 2 (27" x 30"): **Row 1:** With dark yellow, ch 109, rep row 1 as for bright green strip 1.

Rows 2–74: Rep rows 2 and 3 alternately as for bright green strip 1, until piece measures 30" from beg. Fasten off after row 74.

Square (make 1 ea bright blue, bright red, bright green): **Row 1:** Ch 24, rep row 1 as for bright green strip 1.

Rows 2–12: Rep rows 2 and 3 alternately as for bright green strip 1, until piece measures 5" from beg. Fasten off after row 12.

Circle (make 1 ea using colors as foll):

	Rnds 1 and 2	Rnds 3 and 4
A	Bright blue	Dark yellow
B	Hot pink	Bright blue
C	Bright red	Bright green
D	Dark yellow	Bright red
E	Bright blue	Hot pink
F	Bright red	Bright blue

Rnd 1: With first color, ch 4, join with a sl st to form a ring, ch 3 for first dc, 14 dc in ring, sl st in top of beg ch-3 = 15 sts.

Rnd 2: Ch 3 for first dc, dc in same st, 2 dc in ea st around, sl st in top of beg ch-3 = 30 sts. Fasten off.

Rnd 3: Join next color in any st, ch 3 for first dc, dc in same st, * dc in next st, 2 dc in next st, rep from * around, end with sl st in top of beg ch-3 = 45 sts.

Rnd 4: Ch 3 for first dc, dc in next st, * 2 dc in next st, dc in ea of next 2 sts, rep from * around, end with sl st in top of beg ch-3 = 60 sts. Fasten off.

Star (make 3 dark yellow; 1 bright blue): **Rnd 1:** Ch 4, join with a sl st to form a ring, ch 3 for first dc, 14 dc in ring, sl st in top of beg ch-3.

Rnd 2: * Ch 11, sl st in 3rd ch from hook, sc in ea of next 2 ch, hdc in ea of next 2 ch, dc in ea of next 2 ch, tr in ea of next 2 ch (point of star made), sk 2 dc of rnd 1, sl st in next dc, rep from *

4 times more, end with sl st in base of beg ch-11. Fasten off.

Triangle (make 1 bright green): **Row 1:** Ch 4, 4 dc in 4th ch from hook, turn.

Rows 2–8: Ch 3 for first dc, dc in same st, dc in ea st across to last st, 2 dc in last st, turn. Fasten off after row 8.

Assembly: With right sides facing and referring to placement diagram, whipstitch pieces together and stitch squares, circles, stars, and triangle to throw.

Edging: Matching yarn color to edge of ea piece of throw, join yarn with sc in any corner, * sc evenly across to next corner, (sc, ch 1, sc) in corner, rep from * around, end with sl st in first sc.

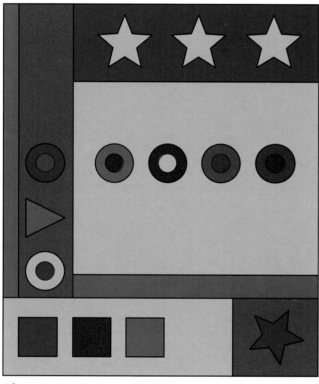

Placement Diagram

Pyramids

Puff stitches lend texture to the simple pyramids that comprise this throw.

FINISHED SIZE
Approximately 43" x 66".

MATERIALS
Worsted-weight acrylic (110-yd. skein): 4 each light dusty green, light dusty pink, light gray; 6 natural; 11 light dusty blue.
Sizes F and G crochet hooks, or size to obtain gauge.

GAUGE
4 hdc and 3 rows = 1" with size G hook.

DIRECTIONS
Note: For all sts, pull up ½" lps.

Triangle (make 22 ea light dusty green, light dusty pink, light gray, light dusty blue, natural): **Row 1** (right side): With size G hook, ch 20, hdc in 3rd ch from hook and ea ch across, turn = 19 sts.

Row 2: Ch 2 for first hdc, pull up a lp in ea of next 2 sts, yo and pull through all 3 lps on hook (sc dec over 2 sts made), * (yo and pull up a lp) 3 times in next st, yo and pull through all 7 lps on hook, ch 1 (puff made), hdc in ea of next 2 sts, rep from * 3 times more, puff in next st, sc dec over next 2 sts, hdc in last st, turn.

Row 3: Ch 2 for first hdc, sc dec over next dec st and puff, (hdc in ea of next 2 hdc, sk next ch-1, hdc in next puff) twice, hdc in ea of next 2 hdc, hdc in next ch-1, hdc in next puff, hdc in ea of next 2 hdc, hdc in next ch-1, sc dec over next puff and next dec st, hdc in last st, turn = 17 sts.

Row 4: Ch 2 for first hdc, sc dec over next 2 sts, puff in next st, hdc in ea of next 9 sts, puff in next st, sc dec over next 2 sts, hdc in last st, turn.

Row 5: Ch 2 for first hdc, sc dec over next 2 sts, hdc in ea of next 11 sts, sc dec over next 2 sts, hdc in last st, turn = 15 sts.

Row 6: Ch 2 for first hdc, sc dec over next 2 sts, puff in next st, hdc in ea of next 7 sts, puff in next st, sc dec over next 2 sts, hdc in last st, turn.

Row 7: Ch 2 for first hdc, sc dec over next 2 sts, hdc in ea of next 9 sts, sc dec over next 2 sts, hdc in last st, turn = 13 sts.

Row 8: Ch 2 for first hdc, sc dec over next 2 sts, puff in next st, hdc in ea of next 5 sts, puff in next

st, sc dec over next 2 sts, hdc in last st, turn.

Row 9: Ch 2 for first hdc, sc dec over next 2 sts, hdc in ea of next 7 sts, sc dec over next 2 sts, hdc in last st, turn = 11 sts.

Row 10: Ch 2 for first hdc, sc dec over next 2 sts, puff in next st, hdc in ea of next 3 sts, puff in next st, sc dec over next 2 sts, hdc in last st, turn.

Row 11: Ch 2 for first hdc, sc dec over next 2 sts, hdc in ea of next 5 sts, sc dec over next 2 sts, hdc in last st, turn = 9 sts.

Row 12: Ch 2 for first hdc, sc dec over next 2 sts, puff in next st, hdc in next st, puff in next st, sc dec over next 2 sts, hdc in last st, turn.

Row 13: Ch 2 for first hdc, sc dec over next 2 sts, hdc in ea of next 3 sts, sc dec over next 2 sts, hdc in last st, turn = 7 sts.

Row 14: Ch 2 for first hdc, sc dec over next 2 sts, puff in next st, sc dec over next 2 sts, hdc in last st, turn.

Row 15: Ch 2 for first hdc, pull up a lp in next st, sk puff, pull up a lp in next st, yo and pull through all 3 lps on hook, hdc in last st, turn.

Row 16: Ch 1, sc dec over next 2 sts. Fasten off.

Half-triangle (make 20): **Row 1:** With size G hook and natural, ch 11, hdc in 3rd ch from hook and ea ch across, turn = 10 sts.

Row 2: Ch 2 for first hdc, pull up a lp in ea of next 2 sts, yo and pull through all 3 lps on hook (sc dec over 2 sts made), hdc in ea of next 7 sts, turn = 9 sts.

Row 3: Ch 2 for first hdc, hdc in ea st across, turn.

Rows 4–16: Rep rows 2 and 3 alternately.

Row 17: Ch 1, sl st in next st. Fasten off.

Assembly: With right sides facing and referring to placement diagram, whipstitch pieces together.

Edging: **Rnd 1:** With right side facing and size F hook, join natural with sl st in any corner, ch 1, * sc across to corner, (sc, ch 1, sc) in corner, end with sl st in beg ch-1. Fasten off.

Rnd 2: With right side facing, join light dusty blue in any corner sp, ch 2 for first hdc, * (hdc in bk lp only of next st, hdc in both lps of next st) across to corner sp, (hdc, ch 1, hdc) in corner sp, rep from * around, end with sl st in top of beg ch-2, turn.

Rnds 3 and 4: Sl st into corner sp, ch 2 for first hdc, * hdc in ea st to corner sp, (hdc, ch 1, hdc) in corner sp, rep from * around, end with sl st in top of beg ch-2, turn.

Rnd 5: Sl st into corner sp, ch 3 for first dc, puff in same sp, * (hdc in ea of next 2 sts, puff in next st) across to 2 sts before corner sp, hdc in ea of next 2 sts, (puff, dc, ch 1, dc, puff) in corner sp, rep from * around, end with sl st in top of beg ch-3, turn.

Rnd 6: Sl st into corner sp, ch 3 for first dc, dc in same sp, * hdc in ea st across to corner sp, (2 dc, ch 1, 2 dc) in corner sp, rep from * around, end with sl st in top of beg ch-3, turn.

Rnds 7–14: Rep rnds 3–6. Fasten off after rnd 14.

Placement Diagram

Pastel Blanket

Working with two colors at a time, crochet these unusual hexagon blocks. Highlight each block with chain-stitch embroidery.

FINISHED SIZE
Approximately 48" x 60".

MATERIALS
Worsted-weight mercerized cotton (70-yd. skein): 18 light seafoam green, 23 light periwinkle blue.

Worsted-weight mercerized cotton (93-yd. skein): 15 dark periwinkle blue, 17 dark seafoam green.

Size H crochet hook, or size to obtain gauge.

GAUGE
7 sc and 8 rows = 2".

DIRECTIONS
Hexagon (make 6 ea using colors as foll):

	Main color (mc)	Contrasting color (cc)
A	Light seafoam green	Dark seamfoam green
B	Light periwinkle blue	Dark periwinkle blue
C	Dark seafoam green	Light seafoam green
D	Dark periwinkle blue	Light periwinkle blue

Row 1 (right side): With mc, ch 22, sc in 2nd ch from hook and ea of next 10 ch, drop mc, join cc, sc in ea of next 10 ch, turn = 21 sts.

Row 2 (wrong side): Ch 1, sc in ea of next 10 sts, drop cc, using mc, sc in ea of next 10 sts, 2 sc in last st, turn = 22 sts.

Row 3: Ch 1, sc in ea of next 13 sts, drop mc, using cc, sc in ea of next 8 sts, 2 sc in last st, turn = 23 sts.

Row 4 and foll even-numbered rows: Ch 1, sc in ea of next 10 sts, drop cc, using mc, sc in ea st across to last st, 2 sc in last st, turn.

Row 5: Ch 1, sc in ea of next 15 sts, drop mc, using cc, sc in ea of next 8 sts, 2 sc in last st, turn = 25 sts.

Row 7: Ch 1, sc in ea of next 17 sts, drop mc, using cc, sc in ea of next 8 sts, 2 sc in last st, turn = 27 sts.

Row 9: Ch 1, sc in ea of next 19 sts, drop mc, using cc, sc in ea of next 8 sts, 2 sc in last st, turn = 29 sts.

Row 11: Ch 1, sc in ea of next 21 sts, drop mc, using cc, sc in ea of next 8 sts, 2 sc in last st, turn = 31 sts.

Row 13: Ch 1, sc in ea of next 23 sts, drop mc, using cc, sc in ea of next 8 sts, 2 sc in last st, turn = 33 sts.

Row 15: Ch 1, sc in ea of next 25 sts, drop mc, using cc, sc in ea of next 8 sts, 2 sc in last st, turn = 35 sts.

Row 17: Ch 1, sc in ea of next 27 sts, drop mc, using cc, sc in ea of next 8 sts, 2 sc in last st, turn = 37 sts.

Row 19: Ch 1, sc in ea of next 29 sts, drop mc, using cc, sc in ea of next 8 sts, 2 sc in last st, turn = 39 sts.

Row 21: Ch 1, sc in ea of next 31 sts, fasten off mc, using cc, sc in ea of next 8 sts, 2 sc in last st, turn = 41 sts. Fasten off cc.

Row 22: Join mc in first st, ch 1, sc in ea of next 30 sts, drop mc, join cc, sc in ea of next 9 sts, pull up a lp in ea of next 2 sts, yo and pull through all lps on hook (sc dec over 2 sts made), turn = 40 sts.

Row 23 and foll odd-numbered rows: Ch 1, sc in ea of next 10 sts, drop cc, using mc, sc in ea st across to last 2 sts, sc dec over last 2 sts, turn.

Row 24: Ch 1, sc in ea of next 28 sts, drop mc, using cc, sc in ea of next 9 sts, sc dec over last 2 sts, turn = 38 sts.

Row 26: Ch 1, sc in ea of next 26 sts, drop mc, using cc, sc in ea of next 9 sts, sc dec over last 2 sts, turn = 36 sts.

Row 28: Ch 1, sc in ea of next 24 sts, drop mc, using cc, sc in ea of next 9 sts, sc dec over last 2 sts, turn = 34 sts.

Row 30: Ch 1, sc in ea of next 22 sts, drop mc, using cc, sc in ea of next 9 sts, sc dec over last 2 sts, turn = 32 sts.

Row 32: Ch 1, sc in ea of next 20 sts, drop mc, using cc, sc in ea of next 9 sts, sc dec over last 2 sts, turn = 30 sts.

Row 34: Ch 1, sc in ea of next 18 sts, drop mc, using cc, sc in ea of next 9 sts, sc dec over last 2 sts, turn = 28 sts.

Row 36: Ch 1, sc in ea of next 16 sts, drop mc, using cc, sc in ea of next 9 sts, sc dec over last 2 sts, turn = 26 sts.

Row 38: Ch 1, sc in ea of next 14 sts, drop mc, using cc, sc in ea of next 9 sts, sc dec over last 2 sts, turn = 24 sts.

Row 40: Ch 1, sc in ea of next 12 sts, drop mc, using cc, sc in ea of next 9 sts, sc dec over last 2 sts, turn = 22 sts.

Row 41: Ch 1, sc in ea of next 10 sts, fasten off cc, using mc, sc in ea of next 10 sts, sc dec over last 2 sts, turn = 21 sts. Fasten off.

Border: Join cc with sl st in top right point of hexagon, ch 1, * work 20 sc across to next point, 2 sc in point st, rep from * around, end with sc in same st as beg, sl st in beg ch-1. Fasten off.

Embroidery: To define color changes on each hexagon, use contrasting color yarn to work surface chain stitches and embroider 1 diamond in center of each hexagon (see photo).

Diamond (make 8 light periwinkle blue, 7 dark periwinkle blue): **Row 1:** Ch 2, 2 sc in 2nd ch from hook, turn.

Row 2: Ch 1, sc in next st, 2 sc in next st, turn.
Row 3: Ch 1, sc in ea of next 2 sc, 2 sc in last st, turn.
Row 4: Ch 1, sc in ea st to last st, 2 sc in last st, turn.
Rows 5–20: Rep row 4, inc 1 st at end of ea row.
Row 21: Ch 1, sc in ea st across, turn.
Row 22: Ch 1, sc in ea st to last 2 sts, pull up a lp in ea of next 2 sts, yo and pull through all lps on hook (sc dec over 2 sts made), turn.
Rows 23–40: Rep row 22, dec 1 st at end of ea row.
Row 41: Ch 1, sc dec over last 2 sts, ch 1. Fasten off.

Half-diamond (make 2 light periwinkle blue, 4 dark periwinkle blue): **Rows 1–21:** Rep rows 1–21 as for diamond. Fasten off.
Trim: Join contrasting color with sl st in last st of row 21, ch 1, sc in ea st across edge. Fasten off.

Side triangle (make 4 light periwinkle blue, 6 dark periwinkle blue): **Row 1:** Ch 2, sc in 2nd ch from hook, turn.

Row 2: Ch 1, 2 sc in next st, turn.
Row 3: Ch 1, sc in ea of next 2 sts, turn.
Row 4: Ch 1, sc in next st, 2 sc in last st, turn.
Row 5: Ch 1, sc in ea st across, turn.
Row 6: Ch 1, sc in ea st across to last st, 2 sc in last st, turn.
Rows 7–18: Rep rows 5 and 6 alternately = 10 sts after row 18.
Row 19: Ch 1, sk next st, sc in ea st across, turn.
Row 20: Ch 1, sc in ea st across, turn.
Rows 21–36: Rep rows 19 and 20 alternately.
Row 37: Ch 1, sc in next st. Fasten off.
Trim: With right side facing and triangle turned to work across long edge, join contrasting color with sl st in side of row 36, sc evenly across long edge. Fasten off.

Assembly: With right sides facing and referring to placement diagram, whipstitch pieces together.

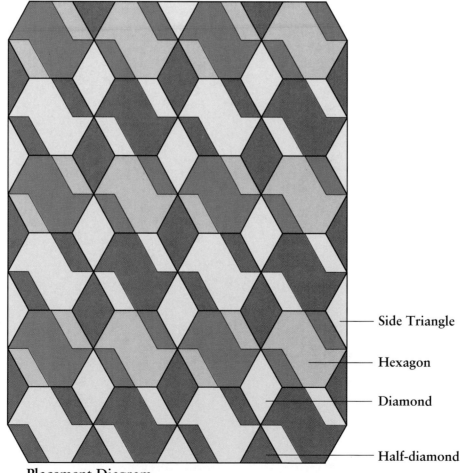

Side Triangle

Hexagon

Diamond

Half-diamond

Placement Diagram

Iris Garden

Here, cross-stitched flowers and crocheted shapes combine to create an eye-pleasing pattern.

FINISHED SIZE
Approximately 55" square.

MATERIALS
Worsted-weight wool (138-yd. skein): 7 light country blue, 11 light taupe, 18 light country green.

Size F crochet hook, or size to obtain gauge.

Size 3 pearl cotton (16-yd. skein): see color key.

GAUGE
5 sc and 6 rows = 1".

DIRECTIONS
Center block (make 4 light taupe, 5 light country green): **Row 1:** Ch 40, sc in 2nd ch from hook and ea ch across, turn = 40 sc.

Rows 2–44: Ch 1, sc in ea st across, turn. Fasten off after row 44.

Triangle (make 16 light country green, 20 light taupe): **Row 1:** Ch 40, sc in 2nd ch from hook and ea ch across, turn = 40 sc.

Row 2: Ch 1, pull up a lp in ea of next 2 sts, yo and pull through all lps on hook (sc dec over 2 sts made), sc in ea st across to last 2 sts, sc dec over last 2 sts, turn = 38 sts.

Row 3: Rep row 2 = 36 sts.

Row 4: Ch 1, sc in ea st across, turn.

Rows 5–28: Rep rows 2–4 = 4 sts after row 28.

Row 29: Ch 1, (sc dec over 2 sts) twice = 2 sts.

Row 30: Ch 1, sc dec over last 2 sts. Fasten off.

Rectangle (make 16 light country blue, 20 light country green): **Row 1:** Ch 64, sc in 2nd ch from hook and ea ch across, turn = 64 sc.

Rows 2–15: Ch 1, sc in ea st across, turn. Fasten off after row 15.

Small block: Make 16 using light country green for first color and light country blue for 2nd color. Make 20 using light taupe for first color and light country green for 2nd color. **Row 1:** With first color, ch 14, sc in 2nd ch from hook and ea of next 11 ch, drop first color, join 2nd color and sc in last ch, turn.

Row 2: Ch 1, sc in next st, drop 2nd color, using first color, sc in ea of next 12 sts, turn.

Rows 3–14: Cont as est working 1 fewer st with first color and 1 more st with 2nd color ea row, turn.

Row 15: With 2nd color, ch 1, sc in ea st across. Fasten off.

Assembly: With right sides facing and referring to placement diagram, whipstitch blocks, triangles, and rectangles together.

Cross-stitch: Using 1 length of pearl cotton, cross-stitch flower design on each center block according to chart.

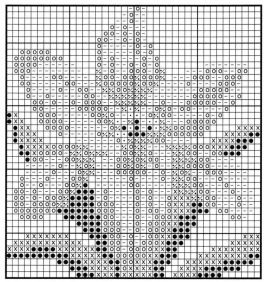

Cross-stitch Chart

Color Key
DMC Size 3 Pearl Cotton
(used for sample)

·	677	Very Light Old Gold (1)
–	754	Light Peach (9)
O	760	Salmon (9)
⅛	3328	Dark Salmon (3)
X	987	Dark Forest Green (4)
●	890	Ultra Dark Pistachio Green (4)

Note: The number of 16-yd. skeins required for each color is indicated in parentheses.

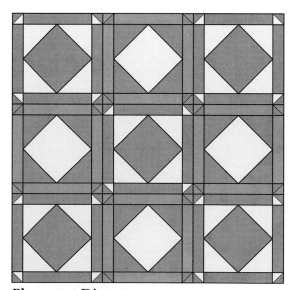

Placement Diagram

Terrific Ts

The origin of the Double T quilt pattern,
tilting cheerfully on this afghan, may
surprise you—it commemorates the
Temperance movement.

FINISHED SIZE
Approximately 51" square.

MATERIALS
Sportweight cotton (120-yd. ball): 5 light peach, 10 variegated cream/peach/blue, 13 light blue.
Size F crochet hook, or size to obtain gauge.

GAUGE
4 hdc and 3 rows = 1".

DIRECTIONS
Two-color square (make the number shown in parentheses using colors as foll):

	Main color (mc)	Contrasting color (cc)
A (40)	Light blue	Variegated
B (80)	Variegated	Light blue
C (40)	Light peach	Light blue
D (20)	Light peach	Variegated

Row 1: With mc, ch 3, 2 hdc in 3rd ch from hook, turn.

Row 2: Ch 2 for first hdc, hdc in same st, hdc in next st, 2 hdc in last st, turn.

Rows 3–6: Ch 2 for first hdc, hdc in same st, hdc in ea st across to last st, 2 hdc in last st, turn. Fasten off after row 6.

Row 7: Join cc with sl st in last st of prev row, ch 2 for first hdc, (yo and pull up a lp) in ea of next 2 sts, yo and pull through all lps on hook (hdc dec over 2 sts made), hdc in ea of next 8 sts, hdc dec over last 2 sts, turn.

Rows 8–11: Ch 2 for first hdc, hdc dec over next 2 sts, hdc in ea st across to last 2 sts, hdc dec over last 2 sts, turn.

Row 12: Ch 2 for first hdc, hdc dec over last 2 sts. Fasten off.

Triangle (make 12 light peach, 28 variegated, 32 light blue): **Rows 1–6:** Rep rows 1–6 as for two-color square. Do not fasten off.

Rows 7–13: Ch 2 for first hdc, hdc in ea st across to last st, 2 hdc in last st, turn. Fasten off after row 13.

Assembly: With right sides facing and referring to T-block diagram, whipstitch matching squares and triangles together to form 36 T-blocks. With right sides facing and referring to placement diagram, whipstitch T-blocks together.

Edging: **Rnd 1:** With right side facing, join light blue with sl st in corner, sc in same corner, * sc across to next corner, (sc, ch 1, sc) in corner, rep from * around, end with sl st in first sc, turn.

Rnd 2: Sl st into corner sp, sc in same sp, * sc in ea st across to corner sp, (sc, ch 1, sc) in corner sp, rep from * around, end with sl st in first sc, turn.

Rnd 3: Sl st into corner sp, ch 3 for first dc, * (dc in next st, sc in next st) across to corner sp, (dc, ch 1, dc) in corner sp, rep from * around, end with sl st in top of beg ch-3, turn.

Rnd 4: Sl st into corner sp, ch 3 for first dc, * (sc in next dc, dc in next sc) across to corner sp, (dc, ch 1, dc) in corner sp, rep from * around, end with sl st in top of beg ch-3, turn.

Rnd 5: Rep rnd 3. Fasten off.

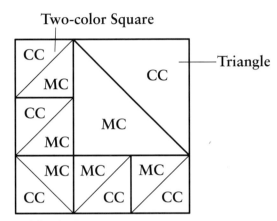

Two-color Square

T-block Diagram

Placement Diagram

Blue & White Nine-patch

The simplicity of this design makes it easy to choose colors to complement your decor. Join crocheted strips of alternating blocks of color to form the check pattern.

FINISHED SIZE
  Approximately 51" x 55".

MATERIALS
  Worsted-weight cotton (109-yd. ball): 13 white, 16 baby blue.
  Size G crochet hook, or size to obtain gauge.

GAUGE
  4 sc and 5 rows = 1".

DIRECTIONS
Strip A (make 10): **Row 1:** With baby blue, ch 11, sc in 2nd ch from hook and ea ch across, turn = 11 sts.
  Rows 2–12: Ch 1, sc in ea st across, turn = 11 sts. Fasten off after row 12.
  Row 13: Join white in last st of prev row, ch 1, sc in ea st across, turn = 11 sts.
  Row 14: Ch 1, (hdc in next st, sc in next st) across, turn = 11 sts.
  Row 15: Ch 1, sc in ea st across, turn.
  Rows 16–22: Rep rows 14 and 15 alternately. Fasten off after row 22.
  Row 23: Join baby blue in last st of prev row, ch 1, sc in ea st across, turn.
  Rows 24–34: Ch 1, sc in ea st across, turn.
  Rows 35–232: Rep rows 13–34 for pat = 11 baby blue squares and 10 white squares. Fasten off after row 232.

Strip B (make 9): **Row 1:** With white, ch 11, sc in 2nd ch from hook and ea ch across, turn.
  Rows 2–10: Rep rows 14–22 as for strip A.
  Rows 11–22: Join baby blue, rep rows 23–34 as for strip A.
  Row 23: Join white, in last st of prev row, ch 1, sc in ea st across, turn.
  Rows 24–230: Rep rows 2–23 as est = 11 white squares and 10 baby blue squares. Fasten off after row 230.

Assembly: With right sides facing and beginning with strip A, whipstitch strips together alternately.

Edging: **Rnd 1:** With right side facing and afghan turned to work across long edge, join baby blue with sl st in corner, ch 1, * work 211 sc across to corner, (sc, ch 1, sc) in corner, work 207 sc across to next corner, (sc, ch 1, sc) in corner, rep from * around, end with sl st in beg ch-1.
  Rnd 2: Sl st backward into corner sp, ch 2 for first hdc, * hdc in ea st to corner sp, (hdc, ch 1, hdc) in corner sp, rep from * around, end with sl st in top of beg ch-2.
  Rnd 3: Sl st backward into corner sp, ch 1, * sc in ea st to corner sp, (sc, ch 1, sc) in corner sp, rep from * around, end with sl st in beg ch-1. Fasten off.

Poppies

A few embroidery stitches transform these crocheted blocks into a field of pretty poppies.

FINISHED SIZE
Approximately 48" x 70".

MATERIALS
Worsted-weight wool-mohair-acrylic blend (146-yd. skein): 2 light country green, 3 dark rose, 4 light yellow, 5 medium rose, 14 light rose.
Size G crochet hook, or size to obtain gauge.

GAUGE
8 sc and 7 rows = 2".
Square = 4".

DIRECTIONS
Square (make the number shown in parentheses using colors as foll):

	Rows 1–4	Rows 5–16
A (96)	Medium rose	Light rose
B (48)	Light country green	Light rose
C (48)	Dark rose	Light yellow

Row 1 (right side): With first color, ch 4, 4 dc in 4th ch from hook, turn.

Row 2: Ch 3 for first dc, dc in same st, dc in ea of next 3 sts, 2 dc in last st, turn = 7 sts.

Row 3: Ch 3 for first dc, 2 dc in same st, (sk next st, 3 dc in next st) 3 times, turn.

Row 4: Ch 3 for first dc, 2 dc in next st, (sk next 2 sts, 3 dc in next st) twice, sk next 2 sts, 2 dc in next st, dc in last st, turn. Fasten off.

Row 5: Join 2nd color in bk lp of last st of prev row, ch 3 for first dc, working in bk lps only, 2 dc in same st, 3 hdc in next st, (sk next 2 sts, 3 sc in next st) twice, sk next 2 sts, 3 hdc in next st, 3 dc in last st, turn = 18 sts.

Row 6: Ch 2 for first hdc, working through both lps, 2 hdc in same st, hdc in ea of next 16 sts, 3 hdc in last st, turn = 22 sts.

Row 7: Ch 1, pull up a lp in ea of next 2 sts, yo and pull through all lps on hook (sc dec over 2 sts made), sc in ea of next 16 sts, sc dec over next 2 sts, sc in last st, turn.

Rows 8–14: Ch 1, sc dec over next 2 sts, sc in ea st to last 3 sts, sc dec over next 2 sts, sc in last st, turn.

Row 15: Ch 1, (sc dec over next 2 sts) twice, sc in last st, turn.

Row 16: Ch 1, pull up a lp in ea of 4 sts, yo and pull through all lps on hook, ch 1. Fasten off.

Assembly: With right sides facing and referring to block diagram, whipstitch squares together. Afghan is 3 blocks wide and 4 blocks long. With right sides facing, whipstitch blocks together.

Edging: Join light rose with sl st in any corner, ch 1, * work 16 sc across edge of each square to corner of afghan, (sc, ch 1, sc) in corner, rep from * around, sl st in beg ch-1. Fasten off.

Embroidery: For flower centers in light yellow section of each block, use a doubled strand of medium rose yarn to make 12 long stitches, ending each stitch with a double-wrapped French knot (see photo).

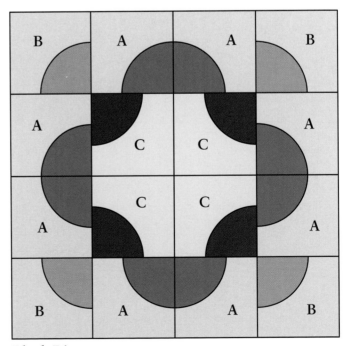

Block Diagram

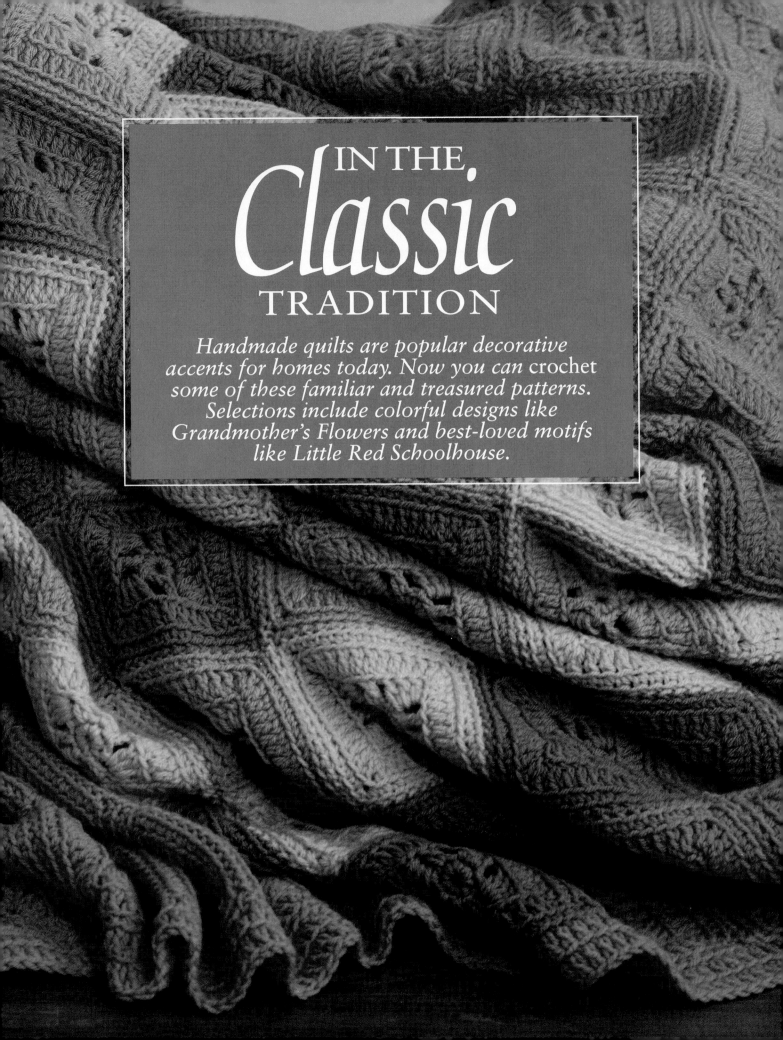

IN THE
Classic
TRADITION

*Handmade quilts are popular decorative
accents for homes today. Now you can crochet
some of these familiar and treasured patterns.
Selections include colorful designs like
Grandmother's Flowers and best-loved motifs
like Little Red Schoolhouse.*

Grandmother's Flowers

*The artful arrangement of the hexagons creates the
flower pattern in this lovely throw.*

FINISHED SIZE
Approximately 58" x 68".

MATERIALS
Worsted-weight cotton (109-yd. ball): 10 cream;
9 dark green; 8 light burgundy; 4 medium burgundy; 3 each mint green, blue; 2 dark purple;
1 dark burgundy.
Size F crochet hook, or size to obtain gauge.

GAUGE
4 hdc and 3 rows = 1".

DIRECTIONS
Hexagon (make 98 cream; 87 dark green; 56 light
burgundy; 23 ea medium burgundy, mint green;

22 blue; 21 dark purple; 10 dark burgundy): **Row
1:** Ch 10, hdc in 3rd ch from hook and ea ch
across, turn = 9 sts.
Row 2: Ch 2, hdc in 2nd ch from hook, hdc in
ea st across to last st, 2 hdc in last st, turn.
Rows 3–5: Rep row 2.
Row 6: Ch 2 for first hdc, yo and pull up a lp in
ea of next 2 sts, yo and pull through all lps on
hook (hdc dec over 2 sts made), hdc in ea st across
to last 2 sts, hdc dec over last 2 sts, turn.
Rows 7–9: Ch 2 for first hdc, hdc dec over next
2 sts, hdc across to last 2 sts, hdc dec over last 2
sts, turn. Fasten off after row 9.

Assembly: With right sides facing and referring to
placement diagram, whipstitch hexagons together.

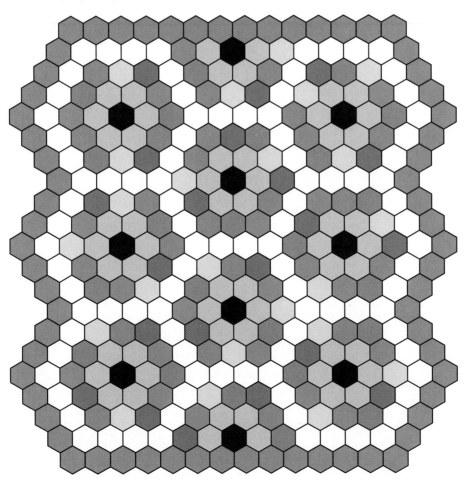

Placement Diagram

Wild Goose Chase

If you are longing to use up balls of yarn left over from other projects, grab your hook and begin work on this afghan.

FINISHED SIZE
Approximately 49" square.

MATERIALS
Worsted-weight cotton (109-yd. ball): 2 each gray, aqua; 3 each mint green, light yellow, baby pink.

Sportweight cotton (120-yd. ball): 2 each light green, tan, light blue; 10 variegated aqua/blue/pink.

Size G crochet hook, or size to obtain gauge.

GAUGE
4 sc and 5 rows = 1".

DIRECTIONS
Two-color square (make the number shown in parentheses using colors as foll):

	First color	Second color
A (18)	Light yellow	Light blue
B (18)	Mint green	Light green
C (18)	Baby pink	Light blue
D (18)	Light blue	Aqua
E (18)	Light yellow	Gray
F (18)	Light yellow	Tan
G (18)	Aqua	Tan
H (18)	Light yellow	Light green
I (18)	Light green	Light blue
J (18)	Baby pink	Tan
K (18)	Baby pink	Aqua
L (18)	Light yellow	Mint green
M (18)	Gray	Baby pink
N (18)	Mint green	Baby pink
O (18)	Mint green	Aqua
P (12)	Gray	Mint green
Q (12)	Light green	Baby pink
R (12)	Mint green	Tan
S (12)	Light blue	Mint green
T (12)	Light yellow	Baby pink
U (12)	Aqua	Light yellow
V (12)	Aqua	Gray
W (12)	Light blue	Gray
X (6)	Light green	Tan
Y (6)	Light green	Gray
Z (6)	Light blue	Tan

Row 1: With first color, ch 8, sc in 2nd ch from hook and ea of next 6 ch, join 2nd color and sc in last ch, turn.

Row 2: Ch 1, sc in next st, drop 2nd color, using first color, sc in ea of next 6 sts, turn.

Row 3: Ch 1, sc in ea of next 4 sts, drop first color, using 2nd color, sc in ea of next 3 sts, turn.

Rows 4–8: Cont as est working 1 more st with 2nd color and 1 fewer st with first color ea row. Fasten off after row 8.

Block Assembly: With right sides facing and referring to photo, whipstitch 6 matching two-color squares together to form each block. Make a total of 64 blocks.

Border: **Row 1:** With wrong side facing and block turned to work across long edge, join variegated yarn with sl st in corner, ch 1, sc in ea of next 23 sts, turn = 24 sts.

Rows 2–4: Ch 1, sc in ea st across, turn. Fasten off.

Rep rows 1–4 across opposite long edge of block.

Assembly: With right sides facing, using colors as desired, and referring to diagram, whipstitch 4 blocks together to form a large block. With right sides facing, whipstitch large blocks together as desired in 4 rows of 4 blocks each.

Edging: **Rnd 1:** With right side facing, join variegated yarn with sl st in any corner, ch 1, * sc in ea st to corner, (sc, ch 1, sc) in corner, end with sl st in beg ch-1.

Rnds 2–9: Sl st backward into ch-1 sp, ch 1, * sc in ea st to corner sp, (sc, ch 1, sc) in corner sp, rep from * around, end with sl st in beg ch-1. Fasten off after rnd 9.

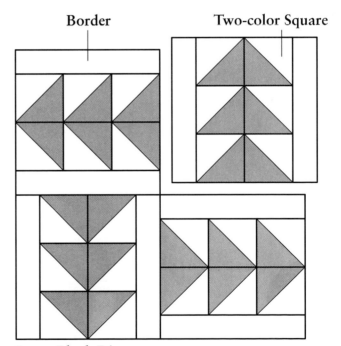

Large Block Diagram

Log Cabin Blues

The pattern for this afghan is one of the most popular and widely made quilt patterns of all time.

FINISHED SIZE
Approximately 69" x 93".

MATERIALS
Sportweight acrylic (175-yd. ball): 14 cream,
15 dark blue, 16 light blue.
Size F crochet hook, or size to obtain gauge.

GAUGE
2 puff sts and 3 rows = 1".
Each strip is 1½" wide.

DIRECTIONS
3" square (make 48): **Row 1:** With light blue, ch
14, sc in 2nd ch from hook, (ch 1, sk next ch, sc in
next ch) across, turn = 7 sc.

Row 2: Ch 2, * (yo and pull up a lp) 4 times in
next ch-1 sp, yo and pull through all lps on hook
(puff made), ch 1, rep from * across, hdc in last st,
turn = 6 puffs.

Row 3: Ch 1, sc in same st, (ch 1, sc in next ch-
1 sp) across, sc in last st, turn.

Rows 4–9: Rep rows 2 and 3 alternately. Fasten
off after row 9.

3" strip (make 48): **Rows 1–5:** With dark blue, rep
rows 1–5 as for 3" square. Fasten off after row 5.

4½" strip (make 96): **Row 1:** With cream, ch 20,
sc in 2nd ch from hook, (ch 1, sk next ch, sc in
next ch) across, turn = 10 sc.

Rows 2–5: Rep rows 2–5 as for 3" square.
Fasten off after row 5.

6" strip (make 48 ea light blue, dark blue): **Row 1:**
Ch 26, sc in 2nd ch from hook, (ch 1, sk next ch,
sc in next ch) across, turn = 13 sc.

Rows 2–5: Rep rows 2–5 as for 3" square.
Fasten off after row 5.

7½" strip (make 96): **Row 1:** With light blue, ch
32, sc in 2nd ch from hook, (ch 1, sk next ch, sc in
next ch) across, turn = 16 sc.

Rows 2–5: Rep rows 2–5 as for 3" square.
Fasten off after row 5.

9" strip (make 48 ea light blue, dark blue): **Row 1:**
Ch 38, sc in 2nd ch from hook, (ch 1, sk next ch,
sc in next ch) across, turn = 19 sc.

Rows 2–5: Rep rows 2–5 as for 3" square.
Fasten off after row 5.

10½" strip (make 96): **Row 1:** With cream, ch 44,
sc in 2nd ch from hook, (ch 1, sk next ch, sc in
next ch) across, turn = 22 sc.

Rows 2–5: Rep rows 2–5 as for 3" square.
Fasten off after row 5.

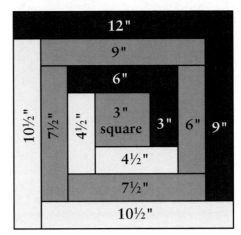

Block Diagram

12" strip (make 48): **Row 1:** With dark blue, ch
50, sc in 2nd ch from hook, (ch 1, sk next ch, sc in
next ch) across, turn = 25 sc.

Rows 2–5: Rep rows 2–5 as for 3" square.
Fasten off after row 5.

Assembly: With right sides facing and referring to
block diagram, whipstitch strips to each square.
Repeat to make 48 log cabin blocks. With right
sides facing and referring to placement diagram,
whipstitch blocks together.

Placement Diagram

Old-fashioned Fans

Frame lacy multicolor fans with a rich rose mohair yarn for this delightful afghan.

FINISHED SIZE
Approximately 40" x 60".

MATERIALS
Worsted-weight wool-mohair-acrylic blend (146-yd. skein): 13 medium rose.

Sportweight wool (900-yd. skein): 1 multicolor rose and mauve.

Size G crochet hook, or size to obtain gauge.

GAUGE
Square = 10".

DIRECTIONS

Square (make 24): **Hub: Row 1:** With rose, ch 4, 4 dc in 4th ch from hook, turn.

Row 2: Ch 3 for first dc, dc in same st, dc in ea of next 3 sts, 2 dc in last st, turn = 7 sts.

Row 3: Ch 3 for first dc, dc in same st, (dc in next st, 2 dc in next st) 3 times, turn = 11 sts.

Row 4: Ch 3 for first dc, dc in same st, 2 dc in next st, (dc in ea of next 3 sts, 2 dc in next st) twice, 2 dc in last st, turn = 16 sts.

Row 5: Ch 1, sc in ea st across. Fasten off.

Vanes: Row 1: Join multicolor yarn with sl st in ft lp of last st of prev row, ch 21, working in ft lps only, tr in 5th ch from hook and ea of next 4 ch, dc in ea of next 5 ch, hdc in ea of next 5 ch, sc in ea of next 2 ch, sl st in ft lp only of ea of next 2 sc on hub, turn.

Row 2: Working through both lps of vane sts, sc in ea of next 2 sts, hdc in ea of next 5 sts, dc in ea of next 5 sts, tr in ea of next 5 sts, turn.

Row 3: Ch 4 for first tr, tr in ea of next 4 sts, dc in ea of next 5 sts, hdc in ea of next 5 sts, sc in ea of next 2 sts, sl st in ft lp only of ea of next 2 sc on hub, turn.

Rows 4–16: Rep rows 2 and 3 alternately.

Shell edging: Work the foll rows across vanes in sides of rows. **Row 17:** Work 7 tr in same st as last tr of prev row, * sl st in last st of next row, 7 tr in last st of next row, rep from * 7 times more, sl st in last st of next row, turn = 8 shells. Fasten off.

Row 18: Join rose with sl st in last sl st of prev row, ch 3 for first dc, 2 dc in same st, [(sc in center tr of next shell, 5-dc shell in next sl st) 3 times, sc in center tr of next shell], 5 tr in next sl st, rep bet [ ] once, sc in center tr of last shell, 3 dc in last st, turn.

Row 19: Ch 3, sl st in next sc, ch 2, sl st in center dc of next shell, ch 2, sc in next sc, ch 2, sc in center dc of next shell, ch 2, hdc in next sc, ch 2, 3 hdc in center dc of next shell, ch 2, 3 tr in next sc, (3 tr, ch 3, 3 tr) in center tr of next shell for corner, 3 tr in next sc, ch 2, 3 hdc in center dc of next shell, ch 2, hdc in next sc, ch 2, sc in center dc of next shell, ch 2, sc in next sc, ch 2, sc in center dc of next shell, ch 2, sl st in next sc, ch 2, sl st in last st, turn.

Row 20: Ch 1, 3 sc in ea of next 3 sps, 3 hdc in ea of next 2 sps, 3 dc in next sp, 3 tr in next sp, tr in ea of next 6 sts, (3 tr, ch 2, 3 tr) in corner sp, tr in ea of next 6 sts, 3 tr in next sp, 3 dc in next sp, 3 hdc in ea of next 2 sps, 3 sc in ea of next 3 sps, sc in last st, turn.

Border: Rnd 1: Ch 1, sc in ea of next 30 sts, (3 sc, ch 1, 3 sc) in corner sp, sc in ea of next 30 sts, [(sc, ch 1, sc) in corner, work 32 sc across to next corner] twice, sc in beg corner, ch 1, sl st in beg ch-1 = 34 sc bet corner sps.

Rnd 2: Sl st backward into corner sp, ch 4 for first dc and ch 1, 2 dc in same sp, * sk next st, dc in next st, sk next st, dc in ea of next 28 sts, sk next st, dc in next st, sk next st, (2 dc, ch 1, 2 dc) in corner sp, rep from * around, end with sl st in 3rd ch of beg ch-4.

Assembly: Afghan is 4 blocks wide and 6 blocks long. With right sides facing and all fans turned the same direction, whipstitch blocks together through bk lps only.

Edging: Join rose with sl st in any corner, ch 3 for first dc, dc in same sp, * dc in ea st to next corner, (2 dc, ch 1, 2 dc) in corner, rep from * around, end with sl st in top of beg ch-3. Fasten off.

Oh My Stars

*Reinterpret this best-loved quilt pattern
with simply stitched squares and triangles—
assembly is easy with our color diagram.*

FINISHED SIZE
Approximately 44" x 55".

MATERIALS
Sportweight acrylic (165-yd. ball): 3 each cream, peach, light aqua, light dusty pink; 6 dark aqua.
Size E crochet hook, or size to obtain gauge.

GAUGE
3 sc and 5 rows in pat = 1".

DIRECTIONS
Large square (make 26 cream; 30 ea peach, light aqua; 32 light dusty pink; 42 dark aqua): **Row 1:** Ch 19, sc in 3rd ch from hook, (ch 1, sk next ch, sc in next ch) 8 times, turn.
   Rows 2–14: Ch 1, (sc in next ch-1 sp, ch 1) 8 times, sc in last sp, turn. Fasten off after row 14.

Small square (make 4 cream; 12 ea peach, light aqua; 16 light dusty pink; 36 dark aqua): **Row 1:** Ch 13, sc in 3rd ch from hook, (ch 1, sk next ch, sc in next ch) 5 times, turn.

Rows 2–9: Ch 1, (sc in next ch-1 sp, ch 1) 5 times, sc in last sp, turn. Fasten off after row 9.

Large triangle (make 16 light dusty pink; 24 ea peach, light aqua; 40 cream; 56 dark aqua): **Row 1:** Ch 2, sc in 2nd ch from hook, turn.
   Row 2: Ch 1, (sc, ch 1, sc) in next st, turn.
   Row 3: Ch 1, sc in next ch-1 sp, ch 1, (sc, ch 1, sc) in last st, turn.
   Rows 4–10: Ch 1, (sc in next ch-1 sp, ch 1) across to last st, (sc, ch 1, sc) in last st, turn.
   Row 11: Ch 1, (sc in next ch-1 sp, ch 1) 9 times, sc in last st. Fasten off.

Small triangle (make 32 ea cream, peach, light aqua, light dusty pink, dark aqua): **Rows 1–6:** Rep rows 1–6 as for large triangle.
   Row 7: Ch 1, (sc in next ch-1 sp, ch 1) 5 times, sc in last st. Fasten off.

Assembly: With right sides facing and referring to placement diagram, whipstitch pieces together.

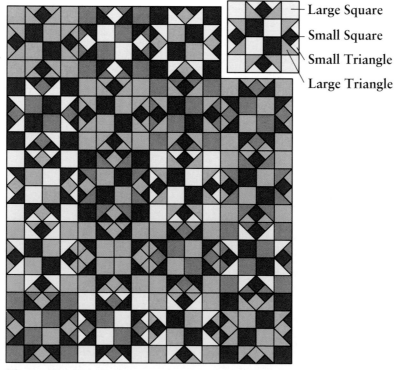

Large Square
Small Square
Small Triangle
Large Triangle

Placement Diagram

Little Red Schoolhouse

The beloved schoolhouse block loses none of
its charm in yarn. Four of the blocks would be
just the right size for a companion pillow.

FINISHED SIZE

Approximately 45" x 60".

MATERIALS

Worsted-weight cotton (109-yd. ball): 10 each brown, light brown; 5 natural; 3 rust; 2 scarlet; 1 gold.

Size E crochet hook, or size to obtain gauge.

GAUGE

4 dc and 2 rows = 1".

DIRECTIONS

Schoolhouse block (make 24): **Section A** (right side): With brown, ch 28, dc in 4th ch from hook and ea ch across = 26 sts. Fasten off.

Section B: Row 1: With right side facing, join rust with sl st in top of first dc of section A, ch 1, sc in ea of next 12 sts, turn.

Rows 2 and 3: Ch 1, sc in ea of next 12 sts, turn.

Section C: Rows 1–6: Ch 1, sc in ea of next 2 sts, turn. Do not fasten off.

Section D: Row 1: Join gold with sl st in next unworked st of section B, ch 1, sc in next st, turn.

Rows 2–6: Ch 1, sc in next st, turn. Fasten off after row 6.

Section E: Row 1: Join rust with sl st in next unworked st of section B, ch 1, sc in ea of next 2 sts, turn.

Rows 2–6: Ch 1, sc in ea of next 2 sts, turn. Fasten off after row 6.

Section F: Rows 1–6: Join gold with sl st in next unworked st of section B and work as for section D. Fasten off after row 6.

Section G: Rows 1–6: Join rust with sl st in next unworked st of section B and work as for section E. Fasten off after row 6.

Section H: Row 1: Pick up rust at edge of section C, ch 1, sc in ea of next 2 rust sts, sc in ea of next 2 gold sts of section D, sc in ea of next 3 rust sts of section E, sc in ea of next 2 gold sts of section F, sc in ea of next 3 rust sts of section G, turn.

Row 2: Ch 1, sc in ea of next 12 sts, turn. Fasten off.

Section I: Row 1: With right side facing, join scarlet with sl st in next unworked st of section A, ch 1, sc in ea of next 4 sts, turn.

Rows 2–9: Ch 1, sc in ea of next 4 sts, turn. Fasten off after row 9.

Section J: Row 1: With right side facing, join light brown with sl st in next unworked st of section A, ch 1, sc in ea of next 2 sts, turn.

Rows 2–9: Ch 1, sc in ea of next 2 sts, turn. Fasten off after row 9.

Section K: Row 1: With right side facing, join scarlet with sl st in next unworked st of section A,

ch 1, sc in ea of next 4 sts, turn.

Rows 2–9: Ch 1, sc in ea of next 4 sts, turn. Do not fasten off.

Section L: Row 1: Ch 1, sc in ea of next 4 scarlet sts, sc in ea of next 3 light brown sts of section J, sc in ea of next 5 scarlet sts of section I, turn.

Row 2: Ch 1, sc in ea of next 13 sts. Fasten off.

Section M: Row 1: With right side facing, join light brown with sl st in st at edge of section H, ch 1, sc in ea of next 12 sts, turn.

Row 2: Ch 1, sc in same st, sc in ea of next 11 sts, turn.

Row 3: Ch 1, sk next st, sc in ea of next 10 sts, 2 sc in last st, turn.

Rows 4–8: Rep rows 2 and 3 alternately. Fasten off after row 8.

Section N: Row 1: With right side facing, join rust with sl st in st at edge of section L, ch 1, sc in ea of next 12 sts, turn.

Row 2: Ch 1, sk next st, sc in ea of next 10 sts, turn.

Row 3: Ch 1, sk next st, sc in ea of next 8 sts, turn.

Row 4: Ch 1, sk next st, sc in ea of next 6 sts, turn.

Row 5: Ch 1, sk next st, sc in ea of next 4 sts, turn.

Row 6: Ch 1, sk next st, sc in ea of next 2 sts, turn.

Row 7: Ch 1, sk next st, sc in next st. Fasten off.

Section O: Row 1: With right side facing, join scarlet with sl st in st at edge of top of section M, ch 1, sc in ea of next 2 sts, turn.

Rows 2–4: Ch 1, sc in ea of next 2 sts, turn. Fasten off after row 4.

Row 5: Join natural with sl st in last row-4 st, ch 1, sc in ea of next 2 sts, turn.

Rows 6–8: Ch 1, sc in ea of next 2 sts, turn. Fasten off after row 8.

Section P: Row 1: With right side facing, join natural with sl st in next unworked st of section M, ch 1, sc in ea of next 6 sts, turn.

Rows 2–8: Ch 1, sc in ea of next 6 sts, turn. Fasten off after row 8.

Section Q: Rows 1–8: With right side facing, join scarlet with sl st in next unworked st of section M and work as for section O.

Section R: Row 1: With right side facing, join natural with sl st in first row-1 st of section M, ch 1, work 8 sc across side edge of section M, turn.

Row 2: Ch 1, sk 1 st, sc in ea of next 7 sts, turn.

Row 3: Ch 1, sk next st, sc in ea of next 6 sts, turn.

Row 4: Ch 1, sk next st, sc in ea of next 5 sts, turn.

Row 5: Ch 1, sk next st, sc in ea of next 4 sts, turn.

Row 6: Ch 1, sk next st, sc in ea of next 3 sts, turn.

Row 7: Ch 1, sk next st, sc in ea of next 2 sts, turn.

Row 8: Ch 1, sk next st, sc in next st, turn.

Row 9: Ch 1, work 6 sc across edge in sides of rows just made, turn.

Rows 10–16: Ch 1, sc in ea of next 6 sts, turn. Fasten off after row 16.

Section S: Row 1: With wrong side facing, join natural with sl st in last row-1 st of section N, ch 1, work 8 sc across side edge of section N, turn.

Rows 2–16: Rep rows 2–16 as for section R. Do not fasten off.

Finishing: Using matching yarn, weave all sections together.

Border: Rnd 1: With right side facing, pick up natural at end of section S, ch 1, * work 25 sc across to corner, (sc, ch 1, sc) in corner, rep from * around, end with sl st in beg ch-1. Fasten off.

Rnd 2: Join brown with sl st in any corner sp, ch 2 for first hdc, * hdc in ea st to corner sp, (hdc, ch 1, hdc) in corner sp, rep from * around, end with sl st in top of beg ch-2.

Rnd 3: Sl st backward into corner sp, ch 1, working in bk lps only, * sc in ea st to corner sp, (sc, ch 1, sc) in corner sp, rep from * around, end with sl st in beg ch-1. Fasten off.

Solid block (make 24 light brown): **Row 1** (right side): Ch 28, dc in 4th ch from hook and ea ch

across, turn = 26 dc.

Rows 2–12: Ch 3 for first dc, dc in ea st across, turn. Fasten off after row 12.

Border: Rnd 1: With right side facing, join brown with sl st in first st of row 12, ch 2 for first hdc, * 2 hdc in next st, hdc in ea of next 9 sts, 2 hdc in next st, hdc in ea of next 11 sts, 2 hdc in next st, (hdc, ch 1, hdc) in corner, work 27 hdc across to next corner, (hdc, ch 1, hdc) in corner, rep from * around, end with sl st in top of beg ch-2.

Rnd 2: Sl st backward into corner ch-1 sp, ch 1, working in bk lps only, * sc in ea st to corner sp, (sc, ch 1, sc) in corner sp, rep from * around, end with sl st in beg ch-1. Fasten off.

Assembly: Afghan is 6 blocks wide and 8 blocks long. With right sides facing, whipstitch blocks together in a checkerboard pattern.

Edging: **Rnd 1:** With right side facing, join brown with sl st in any corner, ch 2 for first hdc, working in bk lps only, * hdc in ea st to corner, (hdc, ch 1, hdc) in corner, rep from * around, end with sl st in top of beg ch-2. Fasten off.

Rnd 2: Join light brown with sl st in corner sp, rep rnd 1. Fasten off.

Rnd 3: Join brown with sl st in corner sp, ch 1, working in bk lps only, * sc in ea st to corner sp, (sc, ch 1, sc) in corner sp, rep from * around, end with sl st in beg ch-1. Fasten off.

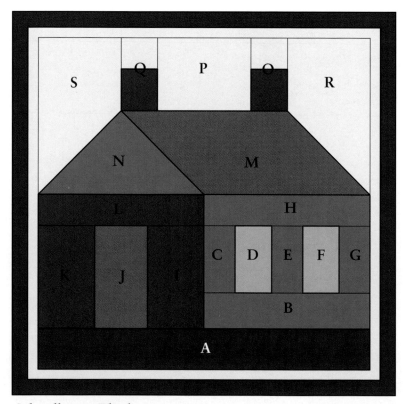

Schoolhouse Block

Honeycomb

You'll find this intricate geometric pattern surprisingly simple to stitch.

FINISHED SIZE

Approximately 50" x 80".

MATERIALS

Worsted-weight cotton (109-yd. ball): 10 each dark aqua, light yellow; 7 white; 6 each medium aqua, light rose, dark rose; 3 medium country purple.

Size G crochet hook, or size to obtain gauge.

GAUGE

4 sc and 4 rows = 1".

DIRECTIONS

Large block (make 15): **Row 1** (right side): With dark aqua, ch 24, sc in 2nd ch from hook and ea ch across, turn = 24 sts.

Rows 2–27: Ch 1, sc in ea st across, turn. Fasten off after row 27.

Small block (make 128 dark rose, 112 medium aqua, 70 light yellow, 60 dark aqua, 40 medium country purple, 28 light rose, 12 white): **Row 1:** Ch 8, sc in 2nd ch from hook and ea ch across, turn = 8 sts.

Rows 2–9: Ch 1, sc in ea st across, turn. Fasten off after row 9.

Two-color block (make the number shown in parentheses using colors as foll):

	Main color (mc)	Contrasting color (cc)
A (56)	Light yellow	Light rose
B (20)	Light yellow	White
C (28)	Light rose	Medium country purple
D (12)	White	Medium country purple

Row 1: With mc, ch 8, sc in 2nd ch from hook and ea ch across, turn = 8 sts.

Row 2: Ch 1, sc in ea of next 6 sts, drop mc, join cc and sc in last st, turn.

Row 3: Ch 1, sc in next st, drop cc, using mc, sc in ea of next 6 sts, turn.

Rows 4–8: Cont as est working 1 fewer st with mc and 1 more st with cc ea row, turn.

Row 9: With cc, ch 1, sc in ea of next 7 sts. Fasten off all yarns.

Small rectangle (make 32): **Row 1:** With light yellow, ch 24, sc in 2nd ch from hook and ea ch across, turn = 24 sts.

Rows 2–9: Ch 1, sc in ea st across, turn. Fasten off after row 9.

Large rectangle (make 6): **Row 1:** With white, ch 40, sc in 2nd ch from hook and ea ch across, turn = 40 sts.

Rows 2–9: Ch 1, sc in ea st across, turn. Fasten off after row 9.

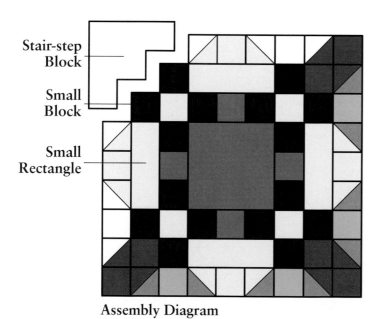

Stair-step Block
Small Block
Small Rectangle

Assembly Diagram

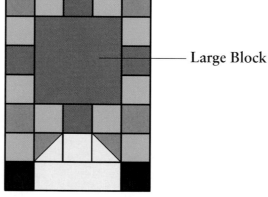

Large Rectangle
Two-color Block
Large Block

Stair-step block (make 4): **Row 1:** With white, ch 24, sc in 2nd ch from hook and ea ch across, turn.

Rows 2–9: Ch 1, sc in ea st across, turn.

Rows 10–18: Ch 1, sc in ea of next 15 sts, turn.

Row 19: Sl st in ea of next 8 sts, ch 1, sc in ea of next 8 sts, turn.

Rows 20–27: Ch 1, sc in ea of next 7 sts, turn. Fasten off after row 27.

Assembly: With right sides facing and referring to diagrams, whipstitch pieces together.

Edging: **Rnd 1:** With right side facing, join white with sl st in any corner, ch 2 for sc and ch 1, sc in same st, * sc in ea st across to corner, (sc, ch 1, sc) in corner, rep from * around, end with sl st in first ch of beg ch-2.

Rnd 2: Sl st into corner sp, ch 2 for sc and ch 1, sc in same sp, * sc in ea st to corner sp, (sc, ch 1, sc) in corner sp, rep from * around, end with sl st in first ch of beg ch-2. Fasten off.

Placement Diagram

Basketweave

*Create an afghan resembling a
finely woven basket from these
quick-to-stitch blocks.*

FINISHED SIZE

Approximately 48" x 54".

MATERIALS

Sportweight acrylic (165-yd. ball): 4 peach;
5 each light dusty pink, light aqua; 6 off-white.
Size F crochet hook, or size to obtain gauge.

GAUGE

9 hdc and 7 rows = 2".

DIRECTIONS

Block (make the number shown in parentheses using colors as foll):

	Main color (mc)	Contrasting color (cc)
A (10)	Light dusty pink	Light aqua
B (10)	Light dusty pink	Peach
C (11)	Light dusty pink	Off-white
D (9)	Peach	Light aqua
E (12)	Peach	Off-white
F (10)	Peach	Light dusty pink
G (11)	Light aqua	Off-white
H (11)	Light aqua	Light dusty pink
I (12)	Light aqua	Peach
J (11)	Off-white	Light dusty pink
K (11)	Off-white	Peach
L (10)	Off-white	Light aqua

Row 1: With mc, ch 19, hdc in 2nd ch from hook
and ea ch across, turn = 18 sts.

Rows 2–4: Ch 2 for first hdc, hdc in ea st
across, turn. Fasten off.

Row 5: Join cc with sl st in last st of prev row,
ch 2 for first hdc, hdc in ea st across, turn.

Rows 6–8: Ch 2 for first hdc, hdc in ea st
across, turn. Fasten off.

Row 9: Join mc with sl st in last st of prev row,
ch 2 for first hdc, hdc in ea st across, turn.

Rows 10–12: Ch 2 for first hdc, hdc in ea st
across, turn. Fasten off after row 12.

Triangle (make 30): **Row 1:** With off-white, ch 3,
work 2 hdc in 3rd ch from hook, turn.

Row 2: Ch 2 for first hdc, hdc in same st, hdc in
next st, 2 hdc in last st, turn.

Rows 3–10: Ch 2 for first hdc, hdc in same st,
hdc in ea st across to last st, 2 hdc in last st, turn.
Fasten off after row 10.

Corner triangle (make 4): **Rows 1–8:** With off-white, rep rows 1–8 as for triangle. Fasten off after
row 8.

Assembly: With right sides facing, referring to photo, and using colors as desired, whipstitch blocks
together beginning at 1 corner and working in diagonal rows. Alternate positioning of blocks to
achieve basketweave effect. Row 1 has 1 block;
row 2, 3 blocks; row 3, 5 blocks; row 4, 7 blocks;
row 5, 9 blocks; row 6, 11 blocks; row 7, 13
blocks; rows 8 and 9, 15 blocks each. After row 9,
use 2 fewer blocks in each row. With right sides
facing and referring to photo, whipstitch triangles
and corner triangles to joined blocks.

Edging: **Rnd 1:** With right side facing and afghan
turned to work across short edge, join off-white
with sl st in corner, ch 3 for first hdc and ch 1, hdc
in same corner, * hdc across to next corner, (hdc,
ch 1, hdc) in corner, rep from * around, end with
sl st in 2nd ch of beg ch-3, sl st into corner sp.

Rnds 2–5: Ch 3 for first hdc and ch 1, hdc in
same corner, * hdc in ea st to corner sp, (hdc, ch 1,
hdc) in corner sp, rep from * around, end with sl
st in 2nd ch of beg ch-3, sl st into corner sp. Fasten
off after rnd 5.

Rnds 6 and 7: Join light dusty pink with sl st in
any corner sp, rep rnd 2. Fasten off after rnd 7.

Rnd 8: Join light aqua with sl st in any corner
sp, rep rnd 2. Fasten off.

Rnds 9–11: Join off-white with sl st in any corner sp, rep rnd 2.

Rnd 12: Ch 1, working in crab st (reverse sc)
from left to right (instead of right to left), sc in ea
st around afghan, sk sts as necessary to keep work
flat, sl st in first sc. Fasten off.

Trip Around the World

*Arrange double crochet-stitch blocks in
concentric circles of color for this cozy throw.*

FINISHED SIZE
Approximately 58" square.

MATERIALS
Worsted-weight acrylic (240-yd. skein): 1 light
purple; 2 each blue, light rose; 3 medium purple;
7 medium rose.
Size H crochet hook, or size to obtain gauge.

GAUGE
4 dc = 1".

DIRECTIONS
Block (make 8 light purple, 17 blue, 20 light rose,
36 medium purple, 88 medium rose): Ch 4, join
with a sl st to form a ring.
Rnd 1: Ch 1, 7 sc in ring, sl st in beg ch-1.
Rnd 2: Ch 4 for first dc and ch 1, dc in next sc,
* ch 3, work 3 dc around post of dc just made, (ch
1, dc in next sc) twice, rep from * around, end
with ch 1, sl st in 3rd ch of beg ch-4.
Rnd 3: Sl st in ea of next 4 ch, ch 4 for first dc
and ch 1, working in bk lps only, dc in same st

(beg corner made), * dc in ea of next 9 sts, (dc, ch
1, dc) in next st for corner, rep from * around, end
with sl st in 3rd ch of beg ch-4.
Rnd 4: Sl st into corner sp, ch 1, working in bk
lps only, * sc in ea st to corner sp, (sc, ch 1, sc) in
corner sp, rep from * around, end with sl st in beg
ch-1. Fasten off.

Assembly: With right sides facing and referring to
placement diagram, whipstitch blocks together
through back loops only.

Edging: **Rnd 1:** Join medium rose with sl st in any
corner, ch 3 for first dc, working in bk lps only,
* dc in ea st across to corner, dc in corner, ch 3,
work 3 dc around post of dc just made, rep from *
around, sl st in top of beg ch-3.
Rnd 2: Ch 3 for first dc, working in bk lps only,
* dc in ea dc across to corner, dc in ea ch of ch-3,
ch 3, work 3 dc around post of dc just made, rep
from * around, end with sl st in top of beg ch-3.
Fasten off.

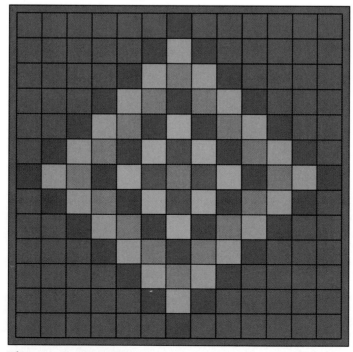

Placement Diagram

Prairie Memories

*Earthy colors and primitive cross-stitch
motifs—reindeer, trees, and houses—recall
antique sampler handiwork.*

FINISHED SIZE

Approximately 45" x 60".

MATERIALS

Worsted-weight wool-mohair-acrylic blend (146-yd. skein): 20 earth brown.

Size H (10"-long) afghan hook, or size to obtain gauge.

Paternayan Persian wool (8-yd. skein): see color key.

Size F crochet hook.

GAUGE

9 sts and 8 rows = 2" in afghan st.

DIRECTIONS

Note: See page 141 for afghan st directions.

Block (make 30): With earth brown and afghan hook, ch 36, work 34 rows afghan st. Sl st in ea vertical bar across. Fasten off.

Cross-stitch: Centering design on block and using 2 strands of wool, cross-stitch each design on each of 3 blocks.

Assembly: Afghan is 5 blocks wide and 6 blocks long. With right sides facing and referring to photo, whipstitch blocks together.

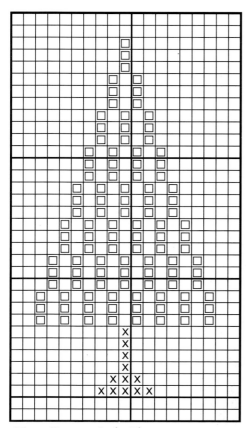

Tree Cross-stitch Chart

Edging: **Rnd 1:** With right side facing and size F hook, join earth brown with sl st in any corner, ch 1, * sc in ea st to next corner, (sc, ch 1, sc) in corner, rep from * around, end with sl st in beg ch-1, turn.

Rnd 2 (wrong side): Sl st into corner sp, ch 1, * sc in ea st across to corner sp, (sc, ch 1, sc) in corner sp, rep from * around, end with sl st in beg ch-1. Fasten off.

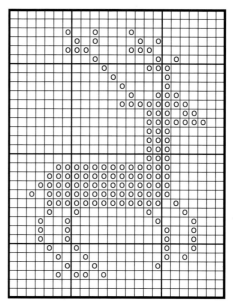

Reindeer Cross-stitch Chart

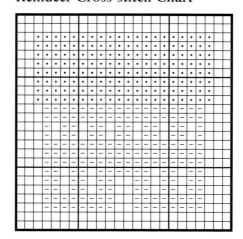

House Cross-stitch Chart

Color Key

Paternayan Persian Wool (used for sample)

·	840	Salmon (3)
O	482	Terra Cotta (4)
□	662	Pine Green (4)
−	464	Light Beige Brown (3)
X	463	Medium Beige Brown (1)

Note: The number of 8-yd. skeins required for each color is indicated in parentheses.

Country Tweed

A tweed yarn—a yarn with light and dark bouclé slubs—adds interesting texture to this ample afghan.

FINISHED SIZE
Approximately 69" square.

MATERIALS
Sportweight cotton-polyester blend bouclé (106-yd. ball): 13 very light taupe; 6 each medium taupe, light tangerine; 5 each terra cotta, medium country purple, light country green; 4 medium aqua; 3 each medium country blue, medium country green.
Size G crochet hook, or size to obtain gauge.

GAUGE
Square = 3".

DIRECTIONS
Square: Make 141 very light taupe (A); 66 medium taupe (B); 61 light tangerine (C); 55 ea terra cotta (D), medium country purple (H); 49 light country green (E); 40 medium aqua (F); 32 medium country blue (G); 30 medium country green (I).
Row 1: Ch 13, sc in 5th ch from hook, (dc in next ch, sc in next ch) 4 times, turn.
Rows 2–6: Ch 3 for first dc, (sc in next dc, dc in next sc) 4 times, sc in last st, turn. Do not turn after row 6.
Border: Ch 1, * sc in ea st to corner, (sc, ch 1, sc) in corner, rep from * around, sc in same st as beg, ch 1, sl st in first sc. Fasten off.

Assembly: With right sides facing and referring to placement diagram, whipstitch squares together.
Optional placement: Assemble very light taupe squares as shown in diagram and all other squares as desired.

B	G	D	H	E	F	B	H	D	G	E	C	B	H	C	E	I	C	H	E	D	B	H
F	A	A	A	A	A	A	A	A	A	A	A	A	A	A	A	A	A	A	A	A	A	E
E	A	C	B	D	C	F	G	E	B	H	D	F	G	D	B	H	F	B	G	C	A	D
B	A	F	G	H	B	I	C	D	F	I	B	E	C	H	F	G	C	D	H	F	A	I
H	A	E	D	C	E	D	B	H	C	E	H	D	B	I	C	D	B	E	B	D	A	E
D	A	C	I	B	A	A	A	A	A	A	A	A	A	A	A	A	C	E	G	A	B	
G	A	B	H	F	A	I	F	C	B	F	D	E	H	F	D	H	A	F	D	C	A	F
E	A	D	E	C	A	D	H	B	I	C	G	B	C	D	G	C	A	B	I	B	A	H
C	A	F	B	G	A	C	G	E	D	H	E	D	I	E	B	I	A	D	H	E	A	I
I	A	C	I	H	A	E	D	C	B	F	A	C	B	H	C	H	A	C	F	B	A	C
D	A	H	E	B	A	I	B	E	G	A	A	A	E	D	E	B	A	E	D	I	A	G
F	A	B	G	D	A	B	F	H	A	A	A	A	B	I	D	A	H	B	C	A	H	
G	A	H	I	F	A	H	C	B	C	A	A	A	H	F	C	E	A	C	G	H	A	E
C	A	E	D	C	A	D	G	D	E	H	A	C	B	D	B	I	A	B	E	F	A	D
D	A	F	B	E	A	C	E	B	C	B	F	E	G	C	F	H	A	D	H	B	A	G
H	A	C	H	I	A	F	H	F	G	D	H	B	E	H	D	C	A	F	C	E	A	F
G	A	B	I	D	A	B	D	C	H	B	E	C	G	B	E	B	A	G	B	D	A	H
D	A	E	F	H	A	A	A	A	A	A	A	A	A	A	A	A	C	H	F	A	I	
F	A	C	G	B	C	G	D	E	C	D	I	B	F	C	B	H	D	E	D	B	A	C
H	A	I	D	E	H	B	D	B	I	H	C	E	H	D	I	C	F	B	G	H	A	G
C	A	B	H	C	I	F	C	H	C	B	D	G	C	F	B	E	H	C	E	I	A	F
D	A	A	A	A	A	A	A	A	A	A	A	A	A	A	A	A	A	A	A	A	A	D
B	H	I	E	D	F	B	G	E	H	C	F	B	D	I	C	G	B	D	H	C	B	E

Placement Diagram

66

Checkered Throw

*By working in afghan stitch, you can fashion
a tightly constructed fabric that is
especially warm.*

FINISHED SIZE
Approximately 37" x 48".

MATERIALS
Worsted-weight wool-mohair-acrylic blend
(146-yd. skein): 5 peach, 12 light country green.
Size G afghan hook, or size to obtain gauge.
Size F crochet hook.

GAUGE
5 sts and 4 rows = 1" in afghan st.

DIRECTIONS
Note: See page 141 for afghan stitch directions.
When changing colors, wrap old yarn over new
yarn so that no holes occur.
Divide peach yarn into 10 small balls. The
checkerboard pattern is worked with separate balls
of peach and green yarns as specified in directions.

Center panel (make 1): **Bottom border: First
checkerboard pat:** With green, ch 133, pull up 7
lps (as specified in row 1, step 1 of afghan st),
* join 1 ball of peach and pull up 7 lps, join another
ball of green and pull up 7 lps, rep from * across =
10 green blocks and 9 peach blocks alternating
across.
Work row 1, step 2 of afghan st, using colors as
est.
Work 4 rows more afghan st (row 2, steps 1 and
2), using colors as est. Fasten off all yarns.
2nd checkerboard pat: With right side facing,
join peach and pull up 7 lps, * join green and pull
up 7 lps, join peach and pull up 7 lps, rep from *
across.
Work 5 rows afghan st, using colors as est.
Fasten off all yarns.
3rd checkerboard pat: With right side facing,
join green and pull up 7 lps, * join peach and pull
up 7 lps, join green and pull up 7 lps, rep from *
across.
Work 5 rows afghan st, using colors as est.
Fasten off all yarns.
4th checkerboard pat: Work as for 2nd checkerboard pat.

Beg body: With right side facing, (join green and
pull up 7 lps, join peach and pull up 7 lps) twice,
join green and pull up 77 lps, (join peach and pull
up 7 lps, join green and pull up 7 lps) twice.
Work 5 rows afghan st, using colors as est.
Fasten off all yarns used for checkerboard pat.
Work 120 rows more afghan st, using green for
center 77 sts and working 4 checkerboard blocks
on ea side, alternating colors as est. Fasten off all
yarns.
Top border: Rep 2nd checkerboard pat. Fasten
off all yarns.
Rep 3rd checkerboard pat. Fasten off all yarns.
Rep 2nd checkerboard pat. Fasten off all yarns.
Rep 3rd checkerboard pat. Fasten off all yarns.

Side panel (make 2): With green, ch 165, work 10
rows afghan st. Fasten off.
Join peach and work 3 rows afghan st. Fasten
off.
Join green and work 5 rows afghan st. Sl st in ea
vertical bar across. Fasten off.

End panel (make 2): With green, ch 133, and
work 18 rows afghan st, changing colors as specified for side panel. Sl st in ea vertical bar across.
Fasten off.

Corner square (make 4): With peach, ch 18, work
18 rows afghan st. Sl st in ea vertical bar across.
Fasten off.

Assembly: With right sides facing and referring to
photo, whipstitch all panels together.

Edging: **Rnd 1:** With size F crochet hook, join
green with sl st in corner, ch 1, * sc across to corner, dec as necessary to keep work flat, (sc, ch 1,
sc) in corner, rep from * around, end with sl st in
beg ch-1.
Rnd 2: Sl st into ch-1 sp, sc in same sp, working
in crab st (reverse sc) from left to right (instead of
right to left), sc in ea st around, sl st in first sc.
Fasten off.

Irish Chain

Join blue and purple nine-patch blocks with solid blue blocks to create a traditional chain pattern.

FINISHED SIZE
Approximately 50" square.

MATERIALS
Worsted-weight cotton (109-yd. ball): 5 light purple.

Sportweight cotton (120-yd. ball): 16 light blue.

Size F crochet hook, or size to obtain gauge.

GAUGE
4 sc and 5 rows = 1".

DIRECTIONS
Nine-patch block (make 41): **Strips 1 and 3** (make 1 ea): **Row 1:** With light purple, ch 7, sc in 2nd ch from hook and ea ch across, turn = 7 sts.

Rows 2–7: Ch 1, sc in ea st across, turn. Fasten off after row 7.

Row 8: Join light blue with sl st in last st of prev row, ch 1, sc in ea st across, turn.

Rows 9–14: Ch 1, sc in ea st across, turn. Fasten off after row 14.

Row 15: Join light purple with sl st in last st of prev row, ch 1, sc in ea st across, turn.

Rows 16–21: Ch 1, sc in ea st across, turn. Fasten off after row 21.

Strip 2 (make 1): **Rows 1–7:** With light blue, rep rows 1–7 as for strip 1.

Rows 8–14: With light purple, rep rows 8–14 as for strip 1.

Rows 15–21: With light blue, rep rows 15–21 as for strip 1.

Block assembly: With right sides facing, whipstitch strips 1–3 together to form 1 nine-patch block. Repeat to make 40 more nine-patch blocks.

Solid block (make 40): **Strips 1–3** (make 1 ea): **Row 1** (right side): With light blue, ch 7, sc in 2nd ch from hook and ea ch across, turn = 7 sts.

Rows 2–7: Ch 1, sc in ea st across, turn.

Row 8 (wrong side): Ch 1, working in ft lps only, sc in ea st across, turn.

Rows 9–14: Ch 1, sc in ea st across, turn.

Row 15 (right side): Ch 1, working in bk lps only, sc in ea st across, turn.

Rows 16–21: Ch 1, sc in ea st across, turn. Fasten off after row 21.

Block assembly: With right sides facing and ridges aligned, whipstitch 3 strips together to form 1 solid block. Repeat to make 39 more solid blocks.

Assembly: Throw is 9 blocks square. With right sides facing, whipstitch nine-patch blocks and solid blocks together in a checkerboard pattern.

Edging: **Rnd 1:** Join light blue with sl st in corner, ch 2 for sc and ch 1, sc in same st, * sc across to next corner, (sc, ch 1, sc) in corner, rep from * around, end with sl st in first ch of beg ch-2, sl st into corner sp, turn.

Rnd 2: Ch 2 for first hdc, hdc in same sp, hdc in ea st across to corner sp, 3 hdc in corner sp, rep from * around, end with sl st in top of beg ch-2, turn.

Rnd 3: Ch 1, sc in same st, * sc in ea st to center corner st, 3 sc in corner st, rep from * around, end with sl st in beg ch-1, turn.

Rnds 4–6: Rep rows 2 and 3 alternately. Fasten off after rnd 6.

Rnd 7: Join light purple with sl st in any corner, working in bk lps only, rep rnd 3. Fasten off.

Rnds 8–11: Join light blue with sl st in any corner, rep rnds 2 and 3 alternately. Do not turn after rnd 11.

Rnd 12: Ch 1, working in crab st (reverse sc) from left to right (instead of right to left), * sc in ea of next 2 sts, sk next st, rep from * around, end with sl st in beg ch-1. Fasten off.

Tumbling Blocks

The interplay of lights and darks in this afghan creates the illusion of movement.

FINISHED SIZE
Approximately 44" x 66".

MATERIALS
Worsted-weight acrylic (240-yd. skein): 2 cream; 4 each light gray, medium gray, dark gray.
Size G crochet hook, or size to obtain gauge.

GAUGE
4 sc and 3 rows = 1".

DIRECTIONS
Diamond (make 98 ea light gray, medium gray, dark gray): **Row 1:** Ch 12, sc in 2nd ch from hook and ea ch across, turn = 12 sts.
Note: Work in ft lps only for rows 2–8.
Row 2: Ch 2, sc in 2nd ch from hook, sc in ea of next 9 sts, pull up a lp in ea of next 2 sts, yo and pull through all lps on hook (sc dec over 2 sts made), leave last st unworked, turn.
Row 3: Ch 1, sc in ea of next 11 sts, turn.
Rows 4–8: Rep rows 2 and 3 alternately, ending after row 2. Fasten off.

Triangle (make 14): **Row 1:** With cream, ch 24, sc dec over 3rd and 4th ch from hook, sc in ea of next 17 ch, sc dec over next 2 ch, hdc in last ch, turn.
Note: Work in ft lps only for rows 2–8.
Row 2: Ch 2, sc dec over next 2 sts, sc in ea of next 14 sts, sc dec over next 2 sts, sk next st, hdc in last st, turn.
Row 3: Ch 2, (sc dec over next 2 sts) twice, sc in ea of next 8 sts, (sc dec over next 2 sts) twice, hdc in last st, turn.
Row 4: Ch 2, (sc dec over next 2 sts) twice, sc in ea of next 4 sts, (sc dec over next 2 sts) twice, hdc in last st, turn.

Row 5: Ch 2, sc dec over next 2 sts, sc in ea of next 4 sts, sc dec over next 2 sts, hdc in last st, turn.
Row 6: Ch 2, (sc dec over next 2 sts) 3 times, hdc in last st, turn.
Row 7: Ch 2, sc dec over next 3 sts, hdc in last st, turn.
Row 8: Ch 1, sc dec over last 2 sts. Fasten off.

Side block (make 12): **Row 1:** With cream, ch 24, sc in 2nd ch from hook and ea ch across, turn = 24 sts.
Note: Work in ft lps only for rows 2–8.
Row 2: Ch 2, sc dec over next 2 sts, sc in ea of next 18 sts, sc dec over next 2 sts, hdc in last st, turn = 22 sts.
Row 3: Ch 1, sc in ea of next 21 sts, turn.
Rows 4–8: Ch 2, sc dec over next 2 sts, sc in ea st across to last 3 sts, sc dec over next 2 sts, hdc in last st, turn. Fasten off.

Assembly: Referring to photo for color placement, whipstitch 1 light gray diamond, 1 medium gray diamond, and 1 dark gray diamond together to form 1 block. Whipstitch blocks together to form 7 rows with 8 blocks and 6 rows with 7 blocks. Whipstitch rows together beginning with 8-block row and alternating 7-block and 8-block rows. Whipstitch triangles in spaces at top and bottom of afghan and side blocks in spaces along sides of afghan.

Edging: With right side facing, join cream with sl st in any corner, ch 1, * sc in ea st to corner, dec as necessary to keep work flat, (sc, ch 1, sc) in corner, rep from * around, end with sl st in beg ch-1. Fasten off.

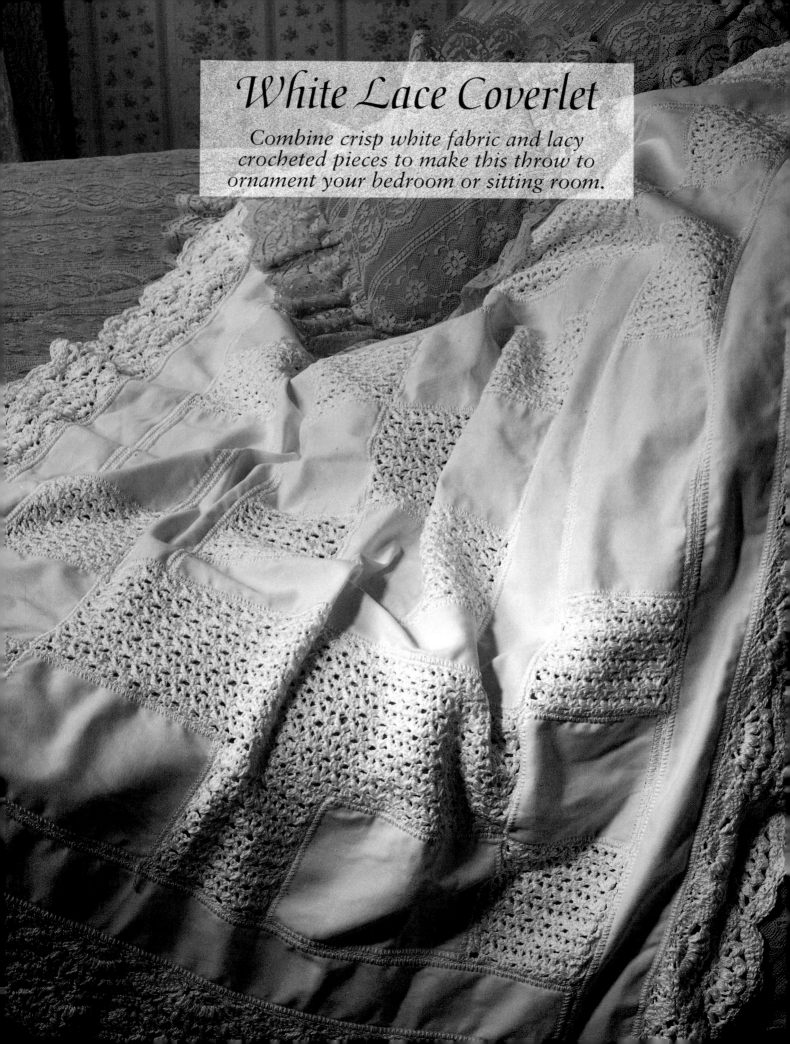

White Lace Coverlet

Combine crisp white fabric and lacy crocheted pieces to make this throw to ornament your bedroom or sitting room.

FINISHED SIZE
Approximately 46" x 56".

MATERIALS
Worsted-weight mercerized cotton (100-yd. skein): 13 white.
Size G crochet hook, or size to obtain gauge.
1½ yards (60"-wide) white sailcloth.
Size 5 crochet cotton (218-yd. ball): 2 white.
Size #7 steel crochet hook.

GAUGE
With size G hook:
2 cl = 1½".
2 cl rows and 1 sc row = 1½".

DIRECTIONS
Block (make 15): **Row 1:** With size G hook and worsted-weight yarn, ch 27, sc in 3rd ch from hook, * ch 3, sk 2 ch, sc in ea of next 2 ch, rep from * 5 times more, turn.

Row 2: Ch 3, (yo and pull up a lp in center ch of next ch-3) twice, yo and pull through all but 2 lps on hook, yo and pull through rem lps on hook (1 leg cl made), ch 1, * dc in same st, ch 1, (yo and pull up a lp) twice in same st **, (yo and pull up a lp) twice in center ch of next ch-3, yo and pull through all but 2 lps on hook, yo and pull through rem lps on hook (cl made), ch 1, rep from * 5 times more, end last rep at **, yo and pull through all but 2 lps on hook, yo and pull through rem lps on hook, ch 1, dc in last st, turn.

Row 3: Ch 1, sc in next st, * ch 3, sk next 2 sts, sc in ea of next 2 sts, rep from * 4 times more, ch 3, sk next 3 sts, sc in ea of last 2 sts, turn.

Rows 4–12: Rep rows 2 and 3 alternately. Fasten off after row 12.

Strip (make 2): **Row 1:** With size G hook and worsted-weight yarn, ch 107, sc in 3rd ch from hook, * ch 3, sk 2 ch, sc in ea of next 2 ch, rep from * 25 times more, turn.

Rows 2–12: Work as for rows 2–12 of block.

Edging: Finished edging is approximately 182" long. **Row 1 (wrong side):** With size G hook and worsted-weight yarn, ch 722, sc in 2nd ch from hook, * sk next 2 ch, 5 dc in next ch (5-dc shell made), sk next 2 ch, sc in next ch, rep from * across, turn.

Row 2 (right side): Ch 3 for first dc, 2 dc in same st, * sk next 2 dc, sc in center dc of next shell, ch 1, work 1 leg cl (as est in row 2 of block) in first dc of next shell, (ch 2, work first leg of next cl in same st, work 2nd leg of cl in next dc of same shell, yo and pull through all but 2 lps on hook, yo and pull through rem lps) 4 times, ch 2, work 1 leg

cl in same st as 2nd leg of last cl, ch 1, sc in center dc of next shell **, 5-dc shell in next sc, rep from * across, end last rep at **, 3 dc in last sc, turn.

Row 3: Ch 1, sc in same st, * work 1 leg cl in top of 1 leg cl, (ch 2, work first leg of next cl in same st, work 2nd leg of cl in top of next cl, yo and pull through all but 2 lps on hook, yo and pull through rem lps) 5 times, ch 2, work 1 leg cl in same st as 2nd leg of last cl **, sc in center dc of next shell, rep from * across, end last rep at **, sc in top of tch, turn.

Row 4: Ch 1, sc in same st, sc in ea st and ch across, do not work in tch, turn.

Row 5: Ch 1, sc in same st, * sk next 3 sc, 5-dc shell in next sc, (sk next 2 sc, sc in next sc, sk next 2 sc, 5-dc shell in next sc) twice, sk next 3 sc, sc in next sc, rep from * across, turn.

Rows 6–9: Rep rows 2–5. Fasten off after row 9.

Assembly: From sailcloth, cut the following: 2 (3½" x 15½") strips, 2 (3½" x 21½") strips, 2 (3½" x 31½") strips, 2 (3½" x 46½") strips, 4 (5½" x 8½") rectangles, 2 (5½" x 11½") rectangles, and 8 (5½") squares. Turn under ¼" around all edges of each piece and hemstitch.

With right side of 1 fabric piece facing and size #7 hook, join size 5 crochet cotton with sc in any corner, * sc evenly across edge to next corner, (sc, ch 1, sc) in corner, rep from * around, end with sl st in first sc. Fasten off. Repeat to work 1 rnd of sc around ea piece. Referring to placement diagram, stitch all crochet (indicated in gray) and fabric pieces together. Stitch crocheted edging to coverlet, easing fullness around corners. Match and whip-stitch ends of edging together.

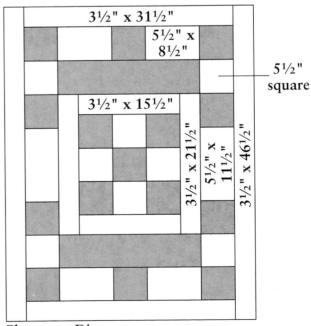

Placement Diagram

BY THE
Fireside

On a cold winter's evening, there's nothing like curling up by the fire with a cozy throw to warm your toes. Keep everyone in your family comfy with afghans chosen just for them and made with love.

Simple Pieces

Use a super-soft yarn in muted colors to crochet triangles, squares, and rectangles for this velvety throw.

FINISHED SIZE
Approximately 56" x 68".

MATERIALS
Worsted-weight wool-mohair-acrylic blend (146-yd. skein): 3 each peach, yellow; 4 light country green; 15 light country blue.

Size G crochet hook, or size to obtain gauge.

GAUGE
4 hdc and 3 rows = 1".

DIRECTIONS
Center panel: **Row 1:** With light country blue, ch 129, hdc in 3rd ch from hook and ea ch across, turn = 128 sts.

Row 2: Ch 2 for first hdc, hdc in ft lp only of next st, (hdc in bk lp only of next st, hdc in ft lp only of next st) across to last st, hdc in last st, turn.

Rows 3–117: Rep row 2. Fasten off after row 117.

Rectangle (make 24 light country blue, 8 light country green): **Row 1:** Ch 44, hdc in 3rd ch from hook and ea ch across, turn = 43 sts.

Rows 2–10: Rep row 2 as for center panel. Fasten off after row 10.

Large square (make 4): **Row 1:** With light country blue, ch 35, hdc in 3rd ch from hook and ea ch across, turn = 34 sts.

Rows 2–20: Rep row 2 as for center panel. Fasten off after row 20.

Small square (make 28): **Row 1:** With yellow, ch 18, hdc in 3rd ch from hook and ea ch across, turn = 17 sts.

Rows 2–10: Rep row 2 as for center panel. Fasten off after row 10.

Large triangle (make 14): **Row 1:** With peach, ch 3, 2 hdc in 3rd ch from hook, turn.

Row 2: Ch 2 for first hdc, hdc in same st, hdc in ft lp only of next st, 2 hdc in last st, turn.

Row 3: Ch 2 for first hdc, hdc in same st, hdc in ft lp only of next st, hdc in bk lp only of next st, hdc in ft lp only of next st, 2 hdc in last st, turn.

Rows 4–21: Ch 2 for first hdc, hdc in same st, (hdc in ft lp only of next st, hdc in bk lp only of next st) across to last st, 2 hdc in last st, turn. Fasten off after row 21.

Small triangle (make 28): **Rows 1–10:** With light country green, rep rows 1–10 as for large triangle. Fasten off after row 10.

Assembly: With right sides facing and referring to placement diagram, whipstitch pieces together.

Placement Diagram

Warm 'n Woolly

*A washable wool yarn is the best choice
for this afghan, which is large enough
to fit a twin bed.*

FINISHED SIZE
Approximately 48" x 92".

MATERIALS
Worsted-weight wool (260-yd. skein): 1 each light rose, teal, light green, dark blue; 2 each rose, medium rose, dark rose, light teal, medium teal, dark teal, green, medium green, dark green, light blue, blue, medium blue.

Size G crochet hook, or size to obtain gauge.

GAUGE
Square = 3½".

DIRECTIONS
Square: Make 8 ea light rose (A), teal (B), light green (C), dark blue (D); 16 ea light teal (E), green (F), medium green (G), light blue (H); 24 ea medium teal (I), dark teal (J), blue (K); 32 ea medium rose (L), dark rose (M), dark green (N); 34 rose (O); 40 medium blue (P). **Row 1** (right side): Ch 15, (sc, hdc, dc) in 3rd ch from hook, * sk 2 ch, (sc, hdc, dc) in next ch, rep from * twice more, sk 2 ch, sc in last ch, turn.

Row 2: Ch 1, (hdc, dc) in same st, * (sc, hdc, dc) in next sc, rep from * twice more, sc in last st, turn.

Rows 3–9: Rep row 2. Do not turn after last row.

Border: Ch 1, working across side edge of square, sc in side of last sc, * work 10 sc across to next corner, (sc, ch 1, sc) in corner, rep from * around, end with sl st in beg ch-1. Fasten off.

Assembly: With right sides facing and referring to placement diagram, whipstitch squares together.

Edging: **Rnd 1:** With right side facing, join dark teal with sl st in corner, ch 2 for first hdc, * hdc in ea st to last st of square, yo and pull up a lp in last st of same square, yo and pull up a lp in first st of next square, yo and pull through all lps on hook (hdc dec over 2 sts made), rep from * across to corner of afghan, (hdc, ch 1, hdc) in corner, rep from * around, end with sl st in top of beg ch-2.

Rnd 2: Sl st backward into corner sp, ch 2 for first hdc, * hdc in ea st to corner sp, (hdc, ch 1, hdc) in corner sp, rep from * around, end with sl st in top of beg ch-2. Fasten off.

J	J	M	N	N	I	I	I	N	N	M	J	J
J	D	M	L	L	K	K	K	L	L	M	D	J
M	M	P	P	P	G	O	O	P	P	P	M	M
N	L	P	B	E	G	H	O	E	B	P	L	N
N	L	P	E	H	F	F	O	H	E	P	L	N
I	K	O	O	O	C	A	C	F	G	G	K	I
I	K	O	H	F	A	O	A	F	H	O	K	I
I	K	G	G	F	C	A	C	O	O	O	K	I
N	L	P	E	H	O	F	F	H	E	P	L	N
N	L	P	B	E	O	H	G	E	B	P	L	N
M	M	P	P	P	O	O	G	P	P	P	M	M
J	D	M	L	L	K	K	K	L	L	M	D	J
J	J	M	N	N	I	I	I	N	N	M	J	J
J	J	M	N	N	I	I	I	N	N	M	J	J
J	D	M	L	L	K	K	K	L	L	M	D	J
M	M	P	P	P	G	O	O	P	P	P	M	M
N	L	P	B	E	G	H	O	E	B	P	L	N
N	L	P	E	H	F	F	O	H	E	P	L	N
I	K	O	O	O	C	A	C	F	G	G	K	I
I	K	O	H	F	A	O	A	F	H	O	K	I
I	K	G	G	F	C	A	C	O	O	O	K	I
N	L	P	E	H	O	F	F	H	E	P	L	N
N	L	P	B	E	O	H	G	E	B	P	L	N
M	M	P	P	P	O	O	G	P	P	P	M	M
J	D	M	L	L	K	K	K	L	L	M	D	J
J	J	M	N	N	I	I	I	N	N	M	J	J

Placement Diagram

Fair Play

*Jazzy blocks punctuated with yellow-and-teal
pinwheels combine in this crocheted
version of a quilt pattern.*

FINISHED SIZE
Approximately 46" x 62".

MATERIALS
Sportweight acrylic (175-yd. ball): 4 red; 2 each
dark green, navy, dark teal, purple; 1 dark yellow.
Size F crochet hook, or size to obtain gauge.

GAUGE
6 sts and 4 rows in pat = 1½".

DIRECTIONS
Block (make 50 red; 14 dark green; 12 ea navy,
dark teal; 11 purple): **Row 1:** Ch 19, hdc in 3rd ch
from hook and ea ch across, turn = 18 sts.

Row 2: Ch 2 for first hdc, 2 hdc in same st, (hdc
in bk lp only of next st, hdc in ft lp only of next st)
8 times, 3 hdc in last st, turn = 22 sts.

Rows 3–12: Ch 2 for first hdc, (hdc in bk lp
only of next st, hdc in ft lp only of next st) 10
times, hdc in last st, turn = 22 sts.

Row 13: Ch 2 for first hdc, working through
both lps, yo and pull up a lp in ea of next 2 sts, yo
and pull through all lps on hook, (hdc in bk lp
only of next st, hdc in ft lp only of next st) 8 times,
yo and pull up a lp in ea of last 3 sts, yo and pull
through all lps on hook, turn = 19 sts.

Row 14: Ch 2 for first hdc, working through
both lps, hdc in ea st across. Fasten off.

Assembly: With right sides facing and referring to
placement diagram, whipstitch blocks together,
leaving 2 rows at each corner of each block
unjoined.

Corner insertion: Use dark teal on red blocks and
dark yellow on all other blocks (see diagram).
With right side facing, join dark teal with sl st in
first unworked st at corner of any red block, ch 3
for first dc, keeping last lp of ea st on hook, work
4 dc across red corner sts, drop dark teal, join
dark yellow, yo and pull through all lps on hook
(beg cl made), working across corner sts of next
block and keeping last lp of ea st on hook, work 5
dc across corner sts, drop dark yellow, pick up
dark teal, yo and pull through all lps on hook (cl
made), cont around rem sts as est, end with sl st in
top of beg cl. Fasten off. Rep to work a corner insertion across unjoined corners of all blocks.

On edges of afghan, work a beg cl on first block
and cl on 2nd block, end with sl st in top of last cl.
Fasten off.

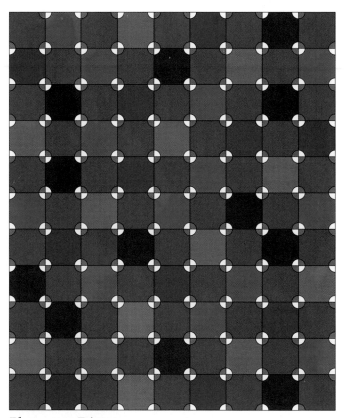

Placement Diagram

Amish Stripes

Rich purple, aqua, and rose framed with dramatic black make this afghan resemble a glowing stained glass window.

FINISHED SIZE
Approximately 60" square.

MATERIALS
Worsted-weight wool (137-yd. skein): 12 black, 6 dark purple, 3 medium aqua.
Worsted-weight wool-mohair-acrylic blend (146-yd. skein): 4 dark rose.
Size G crochet hook, or size to obtain gauge.

GAUGE
4 dc and 3 rows in pat = 2".

DIRECTIONS
Wide strip (make 4): **Row 1** (right side): With dark purple, ch 20, sc in 2nd ch from hook and ea ch across, turn.
Row 2: Ch 3 for first dc, dc in ea st across, turn.
Row 3: Ch 1, sc in ea st across, turn.
Rows 4–91: Rep rows 2 and 3 alternately until piece measures 37" from beg. Fasten off after row 91.

Narrow strip (make 6 dark rose, 3 medium aqua): **Row 1:** Ch 7, rep row 1 as for wide strip.
Rows 2–91: Rep rows 2 and 3 as for wide strip until piece measures 37" from beg. Fasten off after row 91.
Border: With strip turned to work across long edge, join black with sl st in corner, sc in ea st to next corner. Fasten off.
Rep to work 1 border row on ea long edge of ea narrow strip.

Center panel assembly: With right sides facing and referring to placement diagram, whipstitch narrow and wide strips together.
Border: Join black in corner, ch 2 for first hdc, * hdc in ea st to corner, (hdc, ch 1, hdc) in corner, rep from * around, end with sl st in beg ch-2.

Strip A (make 2): **Row 1:** With dark rose, ch 12, rep row 1 as for wide strip.
Rows 2–9: Rep rows 2 and 3 as for wide strip, turn. Fasten off after row 9.
Row 10: Join black, ch 1, sc in ea st across, turn. Fasten off.

Row 11: Join dark purple, ch 1, sc in ea st across, turn.
Rows 12–19: Rep rows 2 and 3 as for wide strip, turn. Fasten off after row 19.
Row 20: Join black, ch 1, sc in ea st across, turn. Fasten off.
Row 21: Join medium aqua, ch 1, sc in ea st across, turn.
Rows 22–29: Rep rows 2 and 3 as for wide strip, turn. Fasten off after row 29.
Row 30: Join black, ch 1, sc in ea st across, turn. Fasten off.
Row 31: Join dark rose, ch 1, sc in ea st across, turn.
Rows 32–109: Rep rows 2–31, ending after last rep of row 19. Fasten off after row 109.

Strip B (make 1): **Row 1:** With medium aqua, ch 12, rep row 1 as for wide strip.
Rows 2–9: Rep rows 2 and 3 as for wide strip, turn. Fasten off after row 9.
Row 10: Join black, ch 1, sc in ea st across, turn. Fasten off.
Row 11: Join dark rose, ch 1, sc in ea st across, turn.
Rows 12–19: Rep rows 2 and 3 as for wide strip, turn. Fasten off after row 19.
Row 20: Join black, ch 1, sc in ea st across, turn. Fasten off.
Row 21: Join dark purple, ch 1, sc in ea st across, turn.
Rows 22–29: Rep rows 2 and 3 as for wide strip, turn. Fasten off after row 29.
Row 30: Join black, ch 1, sc in ea st across, turn. Fasten off.
Row 31: Join medium aqua, ch 1, sc in ea st across, turn.
Rows 32–109: Rep rows 2–31, ending after last rep of row 19. Fasten off after row 109.

Strip C (make 1): **Row 1:** With dark purple, ch 12, rep row 1 as for wide strip.
Rows 2–9: Rep rows 2 and 3 as for wide strip, turn. Fasten off after row 9.
Row 10: Join black, ch 1, sc in ea st across, turn. Fasten off.
Row 11: Join medium aqua, ch 1, sc in ea st

across, turn.

Rows 12–19: Rep rows 2 and 3 as for wide strip, turn. Fasten off after row 19.

Row 20: Join black, ch 1, sc in ea st across, turn. Fasten off.

Row 21: Join dark rose, ch 1, sc in ea st across, turn.

Rows 22–29: Rep rows 2 and 3 as for wide strip, turn. Fasten off after row 29.

Row 30: Join black, ch 1, sc in ea st across, turn. Fasten off.

Row 31: Join dark purple, ch 1, sc in ea st across, turn.

Rows 32–109: Rep rows 2–31, ending after last rep of row 19. Fasten off after row 109.

Edge panel (make 4): **Row 1:** With black, ch 34, rep row 1 as for wide strip.

Rows 2–107: Rep rows 2 and 3 as for wide strip until piece measures 42" from beg. Fasten off after row 107.

Corner block (make 2 ea dark purple, medium aqua): **Row 1:** Ch 34, rep row 1 as for wide strip.

Rows 2–23: Rep rows 2 and 3 as for wide strip until piece measures 8½" from beg. Fasten off after row 23.

Assembly: With right sides facing and referring to placement diagram, whipstitch pieces together.

Edging: Join black in any corner, ch 1, * sc in ea st to corner, (sc, ch 1, sc) in corner, rep from * around, end with sl st in beg ch-1. Fasten off.

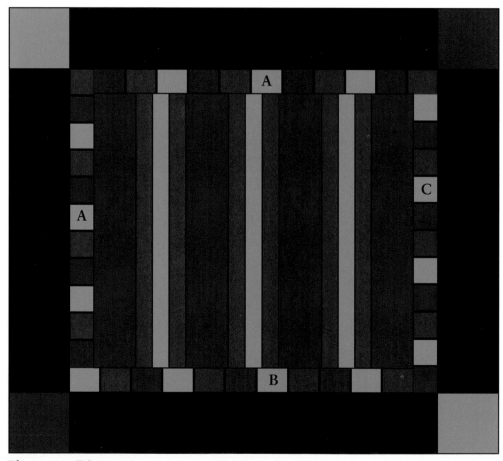

Placement Diagram

A-"Maze" Yourself

You'll be surprised how easy it is to make the unusually shaped pieces that compose this throw.

FINISHED SIZE

Approximately 45" x 52".

MATERIALS

Worsted-weight cotton (109-yd. ball): 8 natural; 5 light brown; 4 each terra cotta, green, brown. Size G crochet hook, or size to obtain gauge.

GAUGE

Large block = 7".

DIRECTIONS

Note: Work all sts in ft lps only.

Large block (make 20): **Row 1:** With natural, ch 33, hdc in 3rd ch from hook, (sk next ch, 2 hdc in next ch) 14 times, sk next ch, hdc in last ch, turn.

Rows 2–17: Ch 2 for first hdc, hdc in next st, (sk next st, 2 hdc in next st) 14 times, sk next st, hdc in last st, turn. Fasten off after row 17.

Cross block (make 12): **Row 1:** With terra cotta, ch 11, hdc in 3rd ch from hook, (sk next ch, 2 hdc in next ch) 3 times, sk next ch, hdc in last ch, turn.

Row 2: Ch 2 for first hdc, hdc in same st, (sk next st, 2 hdc in next st) 3 times, sk next st, hdc in last st, turn.

Row 3: Ch 8, hdc in 3rd ch from hook, (sk next st, 2 hdc in next st) 6 times, drop last lp from hook, join a 12" length of yarn in last st of row 2, ch 6, fasten off, pick up dropped lp and work 2 hdc in last row-2 st, (sk next ch, 2 hdc in next ch) twice, sk next ch, hdc in last ch, turn.

Rows 4–7: Ch 2 for first hdc, hdc in same st, (sk next st, 2 hdc in next st) 9 times, sk next st, hdc in last st, turn.

Row 8: Sl st in ea of first 6 sts, ch 2 for first hdc, hdc in same st, (sk next st, 2 hdc in next st) 3 times, sk next st, hdc in next st, leave rem sts un-worked, turn.

Row 9: Ch 2 for first hdc, hdc in same st, (sk next st, 2 hdc in next st) 3 times, sk next st, hdc in last st. Fasten off.

Half-cross block (make 14): **Rows 1–4:** With terra cotta, rep rows 1–4 as for cross block. Fasten off.

Corner cross block (make 4): **Row 1:** With terra cotta, ch 7, hdc in 3rd ch from hook, sk next ch, 2 hdc in next ch, sk next ch, hdc in last ch, turn.

Row 2: Ch 2 for first hdc, hdc in same st, sk next st, 2 hdc in next st, sk next st, hdc in last st, turn.

Row 3: Ch 8, hdc in 3rd ch from hook, (sk next st, 2 hdc in next st) 4 times, hdc in last st, turn.

Row 4: Ch 2 for first hdc, hdc in same st, (sk next st, 2 hdc in next st) 4 times, sk next st, hdc in last st, turn. Fasten off.

Two-color block (make 31): **Row 1:** With green, ch 19, hdc in 3rd ch from hook, (sk next ch, 2 hdc in next ch) 7 times, sk next ch, hdc in last ch, turn.

Row 2: Ch 2 for first hdc, hdc in same st, (sk next st, 2 hdc in next st) 7 times, sk next st, hdc in last st, turn.

Row 3: Ch 2 for first hdc, hdc in same st, sk next st, 2 hdc in next st, drop green and carry it across by working over it, join light brown and (sk next st, 2 hdc in next st) 5 times, drop light brown and do not carry it across, using green, sk next st, 2 hdc in next st, sk next st, hdc in last st, turn.

Row 4: Ch 2 for first hdc, hdc in same st, sk next st, 2 hdc in next st, drop green and carry it across, using light brown, (sk next st, 2 hdc in next st) 5 times, fasten off light brown, using green, sk next st, 2 hdc in next st, sk next st, hdc in last st, turn.

Rows 5 and 6: Rep row 2. Fasten off after row 6.

Half two-color block (make 18): **Row 1:** With green, ch 11, hdc in 3rd ch from hook, (sk next ch, 2 hdc in next ch) 3 times, sk next ch, hdc in last ch, turn.

Row 2: Ch 2 for first hdc, hdc in same st, (sk next st, 2 hdc in next st) 3 times, sk next st, hdc in last st, turn.

Row 3: Ch 2 for first hdc, hdc in same st, sk next st, 2 hdc in next st, sk next st, hdc in next st, drop green, join light brown and hdc in same st, sk next st, 2 hdc in next st, sk next st, hdc in last st, turn.

Row 4: Ch 2 for first hdc, hdc in same st, sk next st, 2 hdc in next st, sk next st, hdc in next st, fasten off light brown, using green, hdc in same st, sk next st, 2 hdc in next st, sk next st, hdc in last st, turn.

Rows 5 and 6: Rep row 2. Fasten off after row 6.

Zigzag block (make 40 ea brown, light brown): **Row 1:** Ch 11, hdc in 3rd ch from hook, (sk next ch, 2 hdc in next ch) 3 times, sk next ch, hdc in last ch, turn.

Row 2: Ch 2 for first hdc, hdc in same st, (sk next st, 2 hdc in next st) 3 times, sk next st, hdc in last st, turn.

Row 3: Ch 6, hdc in 3rd ch from hook, (sk next st, 2 hdc in next st) 5 times, sk next st, hdc in last st, turn.

Row 4: Ch 2 for first hdc, hdc in same st, (sk next st, 2 hdc in next st) 5 times, sk next st, hdc in last st, turn.

Row 5: Ch 6, hdc in 3rd ch from hook, (sk next st, 2 hdc in next st) 3 times, sk next st, hdc in next st, leave rem sts unworked, turn.

Rows 6–8: Ch 2 for first hdc, hdc in same st, (sk next st, 2 hdc in next st) 3 times, sk next st, hdc in last st, turn. Fasten off after row 8.

Assembly: With right sides facing and referring to placement diagram, whipstitch pieces together.

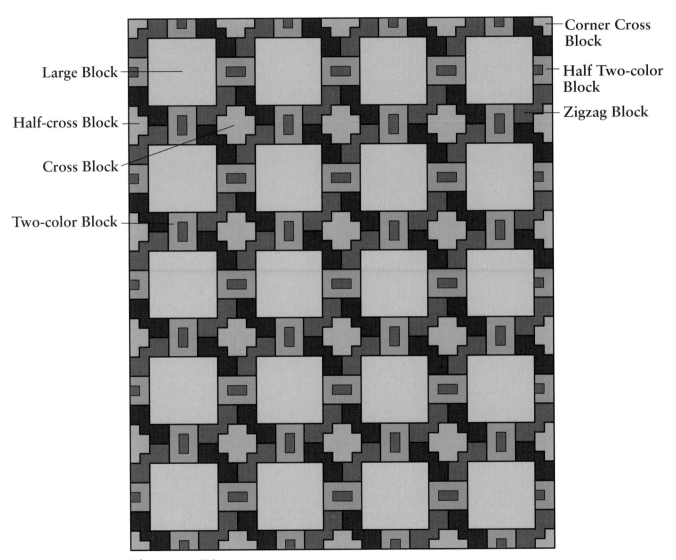

Placement Diagram

Whirling Pinwheels

*Teal pinwheels spin around a
cream-colored background on this
simply elegant afghan.*

FINISHED SIZE
 Approximately 41" square.

MATERIALS
 Worsted-weight wool (138-yd. skein): 9 cream,
8 teal.

Size G crochet hook, or size required to obtain
gauge.

GAUGE
 4 sc and 5 rows = 1".

DIRECTIONS

Block (make 36): **Center triangle** (make 72): **Row 1:** With teal, ch 15, sc in 2nd ch from hook and ea ch across, turn = 15 sts.

Row 2: Ch 1, pull up a lp in ea of next 2 sts, yo and pull through all lps on hook (sc dec over 2 sts made), sc in ea of next 10 sts, sc dec over last 2 sts, turn = 13 sts.

Rows 3 and 4: Ch 1, sc in ea st across, turn = 13 sts.

Row 5: Ch 1, sc dec over first 2 sts, sc in ea st across to last 2 sts, sc dec over last 2 sts, turn.

Rows 6 and 7: Ch 1, sc in ea st across, turn.

Rows 8–15: Rep rows 5–7, ending after 3rd rep of row 6.

Row 16: Ch 1, (sc dec over next 2 sts) twice, turn.

Row 17: Ch 1, pull up a lp in same st as tch and ea of last 2 sts, yo and pull through all lps on hook, turn.

Border: Sc in dec, ch 1, work 20 sc across side of triangle to point, (sc, ch 1, sc) in st at point, sc in ea st across bottom of triangle, (sc, ch 1, sc) in st at point, work 20 sc across side of triangle, sc in same st as beg, ch 1, sl st in first sc. Fasten off.

Side of triangle: Work the foll rows on ea side of ea center triangle. **Row 1:** With right side facing, join cream with sc in bottom right corner of center triangle, sc in ea of next 4 sts, turn.

Row 2: Ch 1, sc in ea st across to last st, 2 sc in last st, turn.

Row 3: Ch 1, sc in ea cream st across, dc in next teal st, hdc in next teal st, sc in ea of next 2 teal sts, turn.

Rows 4–6: Rep rows 2 and 3, alternately.

Row 7: Ch 1, sc in ea cream st across, dc in next teal st, hdc in next teal st, sc in ea of next 3 teal sts, sl st in next teal st, turn.

Row 8: Ch 1, sc in ea st across to last st, (sc, ch 1, sc) in last st for corner, sc in side of ea cream row across to bottom of triangle, sl st in teal corner st. Fasten off.

With wrong side facing, join cream in bottom left corner of center triangle and rep rows 1–8 as est.

Block assembly: With right sides of teal triangles facing, whipstitch 2 triangle pieces together at triangle base to form a block. Repeat to make 35 more blocks.

Assembly: Afghan is 6 blocks square. With right sides facing, referring to photo, and leaving 6 stitches unjoined at each corner of each block, whipstitch blocks together.

Corner insertion: Use teal on cream corners and cream on teal corners. With right side facing, join yarn with sl st in first unworked st at corner of any block, ch 4 for first tr, keeping last lp of ea st on hook, dc in next st, hdc in ea of next 2 sts, dc in next st, tr in next st, yo and pull through all lps on hook (corner cl made), work a corner cl over 6 unworked sts of ea of next 3 blocks. Fasten off, leaving a tail of yarn. Thread tail of yarn through top of ea of 4 corner cl, pull up tightly, and secure to close corner insertion. Rep to work a corner insertion across unjoined corners of all blocks.

On edges of afghan, work a corner cl in ea of 2 blocks, thread tail through top of ea cl, tighten, and secure as est.

To work a cl in ea corner of afghan, join cream with sl st in side of cream st at corner, ch 4 for first tr, keeping last lp of ea st on hook, dc in next st, hdc in ea of next 2 sts, dc in next st, tr in next st, yo and pull through all lps on hook. Fasten off.

Edging: **Rnd 1:** With right side facing, join cream with sl st in top of any corner cl, ch 2 for sc and ch 1, sc in same st, * work 156 sc across to next corner, (sc, ch 1, sc) in corner, rep from * around, end with sl st in first ch of beg ch-2.

Rnd 2: Sl st into corner sp, ch 2 for sc and ch 1, sc in same sp, * sc in ea st to corner sp, (sc, ch 1, sc) in corner sp, rep from * around, end with sl st in first ch of beg ch-2.

Rnd 3: Sl st into corner sp, ch 2 for sc and ch 1, sc in same sp, * sc in ea of next 2 sts, (ch 2, sk 2 sts, sc in ea of next 2 sts) across to corner sp, (sc, ch 1, sc) in corner sp, rep from * around, end with sl st in first ch of beg ch-2. Fasten off.

Rnd 4: Join teal with sl st in any corner sp, ch 2 for sc and ch 1, sc in same sp, * sc in ea of next 2 sc, (working over and around ch-2 lp of prev rnd, dc in ea of next 2 rnd-2 sc, sc in ea of next 2 rnd-4 sc) across to corner sp, (sc, ch 1, sc) in corner sp, rep from * around, end with sl st in first ch of beg ch-2.

Rnd 5: Sl st into corner sp, ch 3 for first dc, 4 dc in same sp, * sc in ea of next 2 sc, (dc in ea of next 2 dc, sc in ea of next 2 sc) across to corner sp, 5 dc in corner sp, rep from * around, end with sl st in top of beg ch-3. Fasten off.

Rnd 6: Join cream with sl st in center st of any corner, ch 2 for sc and ch 1, sc in same st, * sc in ea of next 2 dc, (dc in ea of next 2 sc, sc in ea of next 2 dc) across to center corner st, (sc, ch 1, sc) in center corner st, rep from * around, end with sl st in first ch of beg ch-2.

Rnd 7: Sl st into corner sp, sc in same sp, working in crab st (reverse sc) from left to right (instead of right to left), sc in ea st around, sl st in first sc. Fasten off.

Jewel Diamonds

Diamond blocks made of two-color squares alternate with solid-color blocks for this jewel-tone afghan.

FINISHED SIZE

Approximately 48" x 63".

MATERIALS

Sportweight acrylic (175-yd. ball): 9 burgundy, 5 forest green, 3 navy.

Worsted-weight acrylic (240-yd. skein): 5 navy. Size F crochet hook, or size to obtain gauge.

GAUGE

4 sc and 4 rows = 1" with sportweight yarn.

DIRECTIONS

Small square (make the number shown in parentheses using colors as foll):

	Rows 1–11	Rows 12–22
A (24)	Forest green	Burgundy
B (24)	Burgundy	Forest green
C (16)	Sportweight navy	Burgundy
D (8)	Sportweight navy	Forest green

Row 1: With first color, ch 2, 2 sc in 2nd ch from hook, turn.

Row 2: Ch 1, sc in same st, sc in next st, 2 sc in last st, turn = 5 sts.

Rows 3–11: Ch 1, sc in same st, sc in ea st across to last st, 2 sc in last st, turn = 23 sts after row 11. Fasten off after row 11.

Row 12: With wrong side facing, join next color with sl st in last st of prev row, ch 1, sc in ea of next 20 sts, pull up a lp in ea of last 2 sts, yo and pull through all 3 lps on hook (sc dec over 2 sts made), turn = 21 sts.

Rows 13–21: Ch 1, sk next st, sc in ea st across to last 2 sts, sc dec over last 2 sts, turn.

Row 22: Ch 1, sk next st, sc dec over last 2 sts. Fasten off.

Large square (make 17): **Row 1:** With worsted-weight navy, ch 30, sc in 2nd ch from hook and ea ch across, turn.

Row 2: Ch 1, sc in ea st across, turn.

Row 3: Ch 2 for first hdc, hdc in ea st across, turn.

Row 4: Ch 1, sc in ea st across, turn.

Rows 5–26: Rep rows 2–4 for pat, ending after row 2. Fasten off after row 26.

Assembly: With right sides facing and referring to placement diagram, whipstitch small squares together to form diamond blocks. With right sides facing and referring to placement diagram, whipstitch diamond blocks and large navy squares together.

Edging: **Rnd 1:** With right side facing, join burgundy with sl st in corner, ch 1, * work 29 sc across edge of ea block to corner of afghan, (sc, ch 1, sc) in corner, rep from * around, end with sl st in beg ch-1.

Rnds 2–5: Sl st backward into corner sp, ch 2 for first hdc, * hdc in ea st to corner sp, (hdc, ch 1, hdc) in corner sp, rep from * around, end with sl st in beg ch-2, turn. Fasten off after rnd 5.

Rnd 6: With right side facing, join sportweight navy in any corner sp, ch 2 for first hdc, rep rnd 2. Fasten off.

Rnds 7 and 8: With right side facing, join burgundy in any corner sp, ch 2 for first hdc, rep rnd 2. Do not turn after rnd 8.

Rnd 9: Sl st backward into corner sp, ch 1, * sc in ea st to corner sp, (sc, ch 1, sc) in corner sp, rep from * around, end with sl st in beg ch-1. Fasten off.

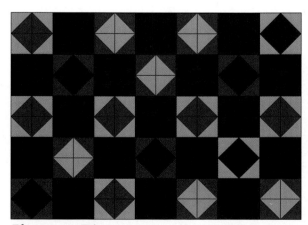

Placement Diagram

Playful Diamonds

Here, diamond blocks are made with lighter, brighter colors and joined with neutral blocks for a variation of the Jewel Diamonds afghan.

FINISHED SIZE
Approximately 48" x 66".

MATERIALS
Worsted-weight acrylic (240-yd. skein): 2 orange, 3 periwinkle blue, 4 rose.

Sportweight acrylic (175-yd. ball): 12 cream.

Sizes F and H hooks, or sizes to obtain gauge.

GAUGE
7 sc and 8 rows = 2" with size F hook and worsted-weight yarn.

6 dc and 3 rows = 2" with size H hook and sportweight yarn.

DIRECTIONS
Small square (make the number shown in parentheses using colors as foll):

	Rows 1–11	Rows 12–22
A (16)	Orange	Rose
B (32)	Periwinkle blue	Rose
C (16)	Rose	Periwinkle blue
D (8)	Orange	Periwinkle blue

Rows 1–22: With size F hook and first color, rep rows 1–22 as for Jewel Diamonds small square (see page 92).

Large square (make 17): With size H hook and 2 strands of cream held tog as 1, ch 4, join with a sl st to form a ring.

Rnd 1: Ch 4 for first dc and ch 1, (3 dc, ch 1) 3 times in ring, 2 dc in ring, sl st in 3rd ch of beg ch-4.

Rnd 2: Sl st into corner sp, ch 4 for first dc and ch 1, 2 dc in same sp, * dc in ea of next 3 dc, (2 dc, ch 1, 2 dc) in next sp for corner, rep from * around, sl st in 3rd ch of beg ch-4.

Rnds 3–6: Sl st into corner sp, ch 4 for first dc and ch 1, 2 dc in same sp, * dc in ea dc to next corner sp, (2 dc, ch 1, 2 dc) in corner, rep from * around, sl st in 3rd ch of beg ch-4. Fasten off.

Assembly: With right sides facing and referring to placement diagram, whipstitch small squares together to form diamond blocks. With right sides facing and referring to placement diagram, whipstitch diamond blocks and large cream squares together.

Edging: **Rnd 1:** With size F hook and 2 strands of yarn held tog as 1, join cream with sl st in any corner, ch 1, * work 25 sc across edge of ea block to corner of afghan, (sc, ch 1, sc) in corner, rep from * around, end with sl st in beg ch-1.

Rnds 2 and 3: Sl st backward in corner sp, ch 4 for first dc and ch 1, working in bk lps only, 2 dc in same sp, * dc in ea st to next corner sp, (2 dc, ch 1, 2 dc) in corner sp, rep from * around, end with sl st in 3rd ch of beg ch-4.

Rnd 4: Ch 1, working in crab st (reverse sc) from left to right (instead of right to left), sc in bk lp only of ea st around, sl st in beg ch-1. Fasten off.

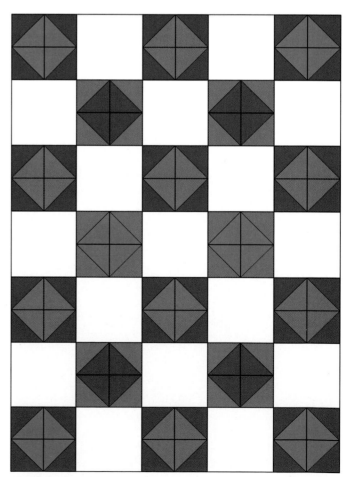

Placement Diagram

Forest of Pines

Stitch together small one- and two-color squares to reveal the Tree of Life quilt pattern.

FINISHED SIZE
Approximately 55" x 74".

MATERIALS
Sportweight acrylic-wool blend (175-yd. ball): 1 dark country blue.

Sportweight acrylic (175-yd. ball): 3 each dark green, brown; 18 ecru.

Size F crochet hook, or size to obtain gauge.

GAUGE
Square = 2".

DIRECTIONS
Solid square (make 54 brown, 550 ecru): **Row 1:** Ch 3, 2 hdc in 3rd ch from hook, turn.

Row 2: Ch 2 for first hdc, hdc in same st, hdc in next st, 2 hdc in last st, turn.

Rows 3–5: Ch 2 for first hdc, hdc in same st, hdc in ea st across to last st, 2 hdc in last st, turn.

Row 6: Ch 2 for first hdc, hdc in ea of next 8 sts, yo and pull up a lp in ea of next 2 sts, yo and pull through all lps on hook (hdc dec over 2 sts made), turn.

Rows 7–9: Ch 2 for first hdc, sk next st, hdc in ea st across to last 2 sts, hdc dec over last 2 sts, turn.

Row 10: Ch 2 for first hdc, sk next st, hdc dec over last 2 sts, ch 1. Fasten off.

Two-color square (make the number shown in parentheses using colors as foll):

	Rows 1–5	Rows 6–10
A (132)	Dark green	Ecru
B (36)	Dark country blue	Ecru
C (36)	Brown	Ecru

Rows 1–5: With first color, rep rows 1–5 as for solid square. Fasten off after row 5.

Rows 6–10: Join 2nd color in last st of prev row, rep rows 6–10 as for solid square. Fasten off after row 10.

Half-square (make 84): **Rows 1–5:** With ecru, rep rows 1–5 as for solid square. Fasten off after row 5.

Assembly: With right sides facing, whipstitch 64 ecru squares together in a 8-square by 8-square block. Repeat to make another solid ecru block. With right sides facing and referring to tree block diagram, whipstitch pieces together to form 6 tree blocks. With right sides facing and referring to triangle diagram, whipstitch pieces together to form 6 triangles. With right sides facing and referring to corner triangle diagram, whipstitch pieces together

to form 4 corner triangles. With right sides facing and referring to placement diagram, whipstitch blocks and triangles together. Whipstitch 1 half-square in place on each long edge of afghan (see placement diagram).

Edging: With right side facing, join ecru with sl st in any corner, ch 2 for first hdc, * hdc in ea st to corner, dec as necessary to keep work flat, (hdc, ch 1, hdc) in corner, rep from * around, end with sl st in top of beg ch-2. Fasten off.

Tree Block Diagram   **Triangle Diagram**

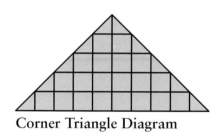

Corner Triangle Diagram

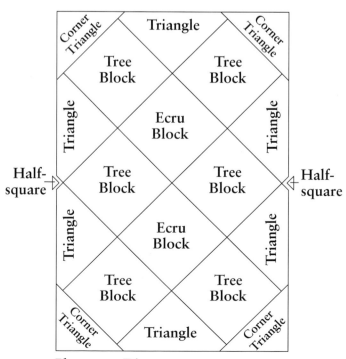

Placement Diagram

Kaleidoscope

*Evoke the shifting patterns of a kaleidoscope
by artfully arranging triangles in a
variety of colors.*

FINISHED SIZE
Approximately 43" x 52".

MATERIALS
Worsted-weight cotton (109-yd. ball): 3 rust; 4 each gold, brown, light brown, green; 7 natural.
Size G crochet hook, or size to obtain gauge.

GAUGE
4 dc and 2 rows = 1".

DIRECTIONS
Large triangle (make 40 ea rust, gold, brown, light brown, green, natural): **Row 1:** Ch 16, dc in 4th ch from hook, dc in ea of next 4 ch, keeping last lp of ea st on hook, dc in ea of next 2 ch, yo and pull through all lps on hook (dc dec over 2 sts made), dc in ea of next 6 ch, turn = 13 sts.

Rows 2–5: Ch 3 for first dc, dc dec over next 2 sts, dc in ea st across to last 3 sts, dc dec over next 2 sts, dc in last st, turn.

Row 6: Ch 3 for first dc, dc dec over next 3 sts, dc in last st, turn = 3 sts.

Row 7: Ch 3 for first dc, dc dec over next 2 sts, ch 1 = 2 sts. Fasten off.

Small triangle (make 4 gold, 5 natural, 6 light brown, 7 green): **Row 1:** Ch 17, dc dec over 5th and 6th ch from hook, (dc in ea of next 3 ch, dc dec over next 2 ch) twice, tr in last ch, turn = 11 sts.

Row 2: Ch 4 for first tr, (dc dec over next 2 sts) twice, dc in next st, (dc dec over next 2 sts) twice, tr in last st, turn = 7 sts.

Row 3: Ch 3 for first dc, dc dec over next 2 sts, dc in next st, dc dec over next 2 sts, dc in last st, turn = 5 sts.

Row 4: Ch 2, pull up a lp in ea of next 3 sts, yo and pull through all lps on hook, hdc in last st, turn = 3 sts.

Row 5: Ch 1, sk next st, sc in last st. Fasten off.

Square (make 4 ea gold, green; 6 ea light brown, natural): **Row 1:** Ch 16, dc in 4th ch from hook and ea ch across, turn = 14 sts.

Rows 2–5: Ch 3 for first dc, dc in ea st across, turn. Fasten off.

Assembly: With right sides facing and referring to placement diagram, whipstitch pieces together.

Edging: **Rnd 1:** With right side facing, join natural with sl st in any corner, ch 1, * sc in ea st across to corner, sk sts as necessary to keep work flat (st count on ea edge, including corner sc sts, needs to be a multiple of 4 sts), (sc, ch 1, sc) in corner, rep from * around, end with sl st in beg ch-1.

Rnd 2: * Ch 3, 3 dc in same st, sk next 3 sts, sl st in next st, rep from * around, end with sl st in base of beg ch-3.

Rnd 3: Sl st in ea ch of next ch-3, turn, ch 3, 3 dc around beg ch-3 of rnd 2, * sk next 3 dc, sl st in next ch-3 sp, ch 3, 3 dc in same sp, rep from * around, end with sl st in same sp as beg ch-3. Fasten off.

**Small
Triangle**   **Large
Triangle**   **Square**

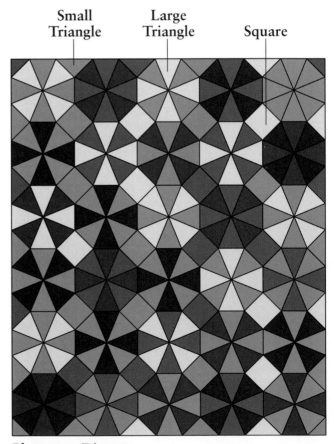

Placement Diagram

Special Effects

Warm earth tones embellished with blue running stitches give this afghan a masculine flavor.

FINISHED SIZE

Approximately 48" x 66".

MATERIALS

Worsted-weight alpaca (199-yd. skein): 11 natural; 8 each medium earth brown, dark earth brown; 4 medium country blue.

Size F crochet hook, or size to obtain gauge.

GAUGE

3 sts and rows in pat = 1".

DIRECTIONS

Large square (make 48): **Row 1** (right side): With natural, ch 24, sc in 2nd ch from hook and ea ch across, turn = 23 sc.

Row 2 (wrong side): Ch 3 for first dc, yo and pull up a lp in same st as tch, yo and pull through 2 lps on hook (first leg of cl made), sk next st, (yo and pull up a lp) 3 times in next st, yo and pull through all 8 lps on hook (cl made), * ch 1, work first leg of cl in same st as last leg of prev cl, sk next st, work 2nd leg of cl in next st, rep from * across, dc in same st as last leg of last cl, turn.

Row 3: Ch 1, sc in ea st across, turn = 23 sc.

Rows 4–19: Rep rows 2 and 3 alternately. Fasten off after row 19.

Small square (make 31): **Row 1** (right side): With medium country blue, ch 16, sc in 2nd ch from hook and ea ch across = 15 sc.

Rows 2–11: Rep rows 2 and 3 alternately as for large square. Fasten off after row 11.

Short strip A (make 48): **Row 1** (right side): With dark earth brown, ch 24, sc in 2nd ch from hook and ea ch across, turn = 23 sc, turn.

Row 2 (wrong side): Sl st in next st, ch 3 for first dc, (work first leg of cl in same st as prev st, sk next st, work 2nd leg of cl in next st, ch 1) 10 times, work first leg of last cl in same st as 2nd leg of prev cl, work 2nd leg of cl in last st, dc in same st as last leg of last cl, turn.

Row 3: Ch 1, 2 sc in same st, sc in ea st across to last st, sk last st, turn.

Rows 4–9: Rep rows 2 and 3 alternately. Fasten off after row 9.

Short strip B (make 48): **Row 1** (right side): With medium earth brown, ch 24, sc in 2nd ch from hook and ea ch across, turn = 23 sc.

Row 2 (wrong side): Ch 3 for first dc, work first leg of cl in same st, work 2nd leg of cl in next st, (ch 1, work first leg of cl in same st as 2nd leg of prev cl, sk next st, work 2nd leg of cl in next st) 10 times, dc in same st as last leg of last cl, sk last st, turn.

Row 3: Sl st in next st, ch 1, sc in ea st across to last st, 2 sc in last st, turn.

Rows 4–9: Rep rows 2 and 3 alternately. Fasten off after row 9.

Large border strip (make 5 ea medium earth brown, dark earth brown): **Row 1** (right side): Ch 48, sc in 2nd ch from hook and ea ch across, turn = 47 sc.

Row 2 (wrong side): Ch 3 for first dc, work first leg of cl in same st as tch, work 2nd leg of cl in next st, (ch 1, work first leg of cl in same st as 2nd leg of prev cl, sk next st, work 2nd leg of cl in next st) 22 times, ch 1, work first leg of cl in same st as 2nd leg of prev cl, work 2nd leg of cl in last st, dc in same st as last leg of last cl, turn.

Row 3: Ch 1, 2 sc in same st, sc in ea st across to last st, 2 sc in last st, turn.

Rows 4–9: Rep rows 2 and 3 alternately. Fasten off after row 9.

Small border strip (make 4 ea dark earth brown, medium earth brown): **Row 1:** Ch 24, sc in 2nd ch from hook and ea ch across, turn = 23 sc.

Rows 2–9: Rep rows 2 and 3 alternately as for large border strip. Fasten off after row 9.

Assembly: With right sides facing and referring to placement diagram, whipstitch pieces together.

Embroidery: Using 2 strands of medium country blue, make running stitches diagonally across large squares as shown in diagram.

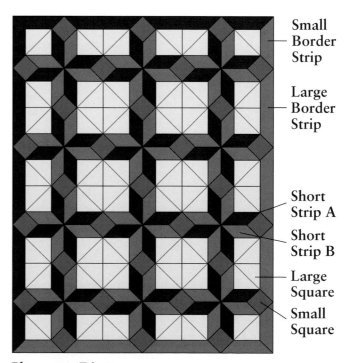

Placement Diagram

Small Border Strip

Large Border Strip

Short Strip A

Short Strip B

Large Square

Small Square

Fancy Fencing

*Comforting colors arranged in a zigzag
pattern offer a cozy escape from
everyday cares.*

FINISHED SIZE
Approximately 53" square.

MATERIALS
Worsted-weight acrylic (240-yd. skein): 3 each
cream, blue; 4 medium rose; 5 dark rose.
Size G crochet hook, or size to obtain gauge.

GAUGE
2 cross sts and 2 rows = 1".

DIRECTIONS
Block (make 49): **Row 1** (wrong side): With dark
rose, ch 32, hdc in 5th ch from hook, working
backward in front of prev hdc, hdc in ch before
first hdc, [sk next ch, hdc in next ch, working
backward in front of prev hdc, hdc in sk ch (cross
st made)] 13 times, hdc in last st, turn = 14 cross
sts.

Row 2 (right side): Ch 2 for first hdc, (cross st
over next 2 sts) 14 times, hdc in last st.

Rows 3 and 4: Rep row 2. At end of row 4, join
blue and work last yo of last st with blue and dark
rose held tog as 1. Fasten off dark rose.

Rows 5–8: With blue, rep row 2, joining cream
at end of row 8 as est in row 4. Fasten off blue after row 8.

Rows 9–12: With cream, rep row 2, joining
medium rose at end of row 12 as est in row 4.
Fasten off cream after row 12.

Rows 13–16: With medium rose, rep row 2.
Fasten off after row 16.

Assembly: With right sides facing and referring to
placement diagram, whipstitch all blocks together.

Edging: **Rnd 1**: With right side facing, join dark
rose with sc in top left-hand corner of afghan,
working in sides of rows of first block, [(sc in side
of next row, 2 sc in side of next row) 8 times = 24

sts across block, * sc in ea of next 2 sts, pull up a
lp in ea of next 2 sts, yo and pull through all lps
on hook (sc dec over 2 sts made), sc in next st, sc
dec over next 2 sts, rep from * 3 times more, sc in
ea of last 2 sts = 22 sts across block] across to corner, (sc, ch 1, sc) in corner, cont around afghan as
est, end with sl st in first sc.

Rnd 2: Ch 2 for first hdc, * (cross st over next 2
sts) to st before corner sp, hdc in next st, (hdc, ch
1, hdc) in corner sp, rep from * around, end with
sl st in top of beg ch-2.

Rnd 3: Ch 2 for first hdc, * hdc in ea st to corner sp, 3 hdc in corner sp, end with sl st in top of
beg ch-2. Fasten off.

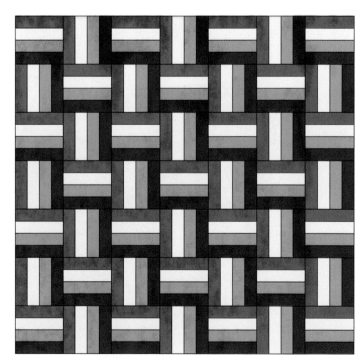

Placement Diagram

Fade to Black

*For this contemporary throw, crochet shades
of gray in a variety of patterns.*

FINISHED SIZE
Approximately 51" x 67".

MATERIALS
Worsted-weight acrylic (240-yd. skein): 3 each
dark gray, medium gray; 5 light gray.
Size G crochet hook, or size to obtain gauge.

GAUGE
Square = 4".

DIRECTIONS
Solid square 1 (make 48): **Row 1:** With dark gray,
ch 15, sc in 4th ch from hook, (dc in next ch, sc in
next ch) across, turn = 13 sts.
  Row 2: Ch 1, (dc in next sc, sc in next dc)
across, turn.
  Row 3: Ch 3 for first dc, (sc in next dc, dc in
next sc) across, turn.
  Rows 4–10: Rep rows 2 and 3 alternately. Do
not turn after row 10.
  Border: Ch 1, sc in same st, * work 11 sc across
to next corner, (sc, ch 1, sc) in corner, rep from *
around, end with sl st in first sc. Fasten off.

Solid square 2 (make 36): **Rows 1–10:** With medium gray, rep rows 1–10 as for solid square 1.
  Border: Work as for solid square 1.

Striped square 3 (make 60): **Row 1:** With medium
gray, ch 13, sc in 2nd ch from hook and ea ch
across, turn = 13 sts.
  Row 2: Join light gray and carry medium gray
across by working over it, ch 1, sc in ea st across,
turn.
  Row 3: Carrying light gray across and working
with medium gray, ch 1, sc in ea st across, turn.
  Row 4: Carrying medium gray across and working with light gray, ch 1, sc in ea st across, turn.
  Rows 5–12: Rep rows 3 and 4 alternately. Do
not turn after row 12.
  Border: With light gray, ch 1, [work 11 sc across
to next corner, (sc, ch 1, sc) in corner] twice, work
11 sc across to next corner, ch 1, sl st in first row-
12 sc. Fasten off.

Zigzag square 4 (make 36): *Note:* To change colors, yo and pull through last 2 lps of st with new
color. Carry yarn not in use across the row by
working over it.
  Row 1: With light gray, ch 15, 2 dc in 3rd ch
from hook, sk next ch, join dark gray in next ch
and carry light gray across, using dark gray, sc in
same ch, * carrying dark gray and using light gray,
sk next ch, 3 dc in next ch (shell made), carrying
light gray and using dark gray, sk next ch, sc in
next ch, rep from * across, turn.
  Row 2: Carrying light gray and using dark gray,
ch 1, sc in center dc of first shell, * carrying dark
gray and using light gray, shell in next sc, carrying
light gray and using dark gray, sc in center dc of
next shell, rep from * across, turn.
  Row 3: Carrying dark gray and using light gray,
ch 3 for first dc, 2 dc in same st, * carrying light
gray and using dark gray, sc in center dc of next
shell, carrying dark gray and using light gray, shell
in next sc, rep from * across, turn.
  Rows 4–7: Rep rows 2 and 3 alternately. Do not
turn after row 7. Fasten off dark gray.
  Border: With light gray, work border as for solid
square 1. Fasten off.

Diamond square 5 (make 12): *Note:* Carry yarn
not in use across the row by working over it.
  Row 1: With dark gray, ch 15, sc in 2nd ch from
hook and ea of next 2 ch, carrying dark gray
across, join light gray with sc in next ch, (carrying
light gray and using dark gray, sc in ea of next 3
ch, carrying dark gray and using light gray, sc in
next ch) twice, carrying light gray and using dark
gray, sc in ea of last 2 ch, turn.
  Row 2: With dark gray, ch 1, sc in same st, (carrying dark gray and using light gray, sc in ea of
next 3 sts, carrying light gray and using dark gray,
sc in next st) 3 times, sc in last st, turn.
  Row 3: Carrying dark gray and using light gray,
ch 1, sc in ea st across, turn.
  Row 4: Rep row 2.
  Row 5: Carrying light gray and using dark gray,
ch 1, sc in same st and in next st, * carrying dark
gray and using light gray, sc in next st, carrying

light gray and using dark gray, sc in ea of next 3 sts, rep from * across, turn.

Row 6: Carrying light gray and using dark gray, ch 1, sc in ea st across, turn.

Row 7: Rep row 5.

Rows 8–12: Rep rows 2–6. Fasten off light gray after row 11. Do not turn after row 12.

Border: Work as for striped square 3.

Assembly: With right sides facing and referring to placement diagram, whipstitch squares together.

Edging: **Rnd 1:** With right side facing, join dark gray with hdc in corner, * hdc in ea st across to last st of square, yo and pull up a lp in last st of same square, yo and pull up a lp in first st of next square, yo and pull through all lps on hook (hdc dec over 2 sts made), rep from * across to corner of afghan, (hdc, ch 1, hdc) in corner, rep from * around, end with sl st in first hdc.

Rnds 2 and 3: Sl st backward into ch-1 sp, ch 2 for first hdc, * hdc in ea st to next corner sp, (hdc, ch 1, hdc) in corner sp, rep from * around, end with sl st in top of beg ch-2. Fasten off after rnd 3.

Placement Diagram

Classic Patchwork

This textured square is so easy to make, you will be crocheting everywhere you go.

FINISHED SIZE
Approximately 50" x 65".

MATERIALS
Worsted-weight mercerized cotton (70-yd. skein): 9 light green; 7 each tan, cream; 6 light purple; 5 medium terra cotta; 3 each light taupe, dark red, dark gold; 2 each medium gold, dark plum, dark purple; 1 each olive green, light blue, dark gray, medium blue, medium rose, light peach.
Size E crochet hook, or size to obtain gauge.

GAUGE
Square = 3½".

DIRECTIONS
Square (make 28 ea light green, light purple; 22 cream; 15 light taupe; 10 ea medium terra cotta, medium gold, dark red; 8 dark plum; 7 tan; 6 dark purple; 5 ea olive green, light blue, dark gray, medium blue, medium rose, light peach; 2 dark gold): **Row 1:** Ch 16, hdc in 3rd ch from hook and ea ch across, turn = 15 sts.

Rows 2–9: Ch 2 for first hdc, hdc in ea st across, turn. Fasten off after row 9.

Assembly: Afghan is 11 squares wide and 16 squares long. With right sides facing, whipstitch squares together as desired.

Edging: **Rnd 1:** With right side facing and afghan turned to work across short edge, join light green with sl st in corner, ch 2 for first hdc, * hdc in ea of next 12 sts, yo and pull up a lp in last st of same square, yo and pull up a lp in first st of next square, yo and pull through all lps on hook (hdc dec over 2 sts made), rep from * 9 times more, hdc in ea of next 12 sts, (hdc, ch 1, hdc) in corner of afghan, [work 12 hdc across side edge of square, hdc dec over last st of same square and first st of next square] 15 times, 12 hdc across side edge of next square, (hdc, ch 1, hdc) in corner of afghan, rep from * around, end with sl st in top of beg ch-2.

Rnds 2 and 3: Sl st backward into corner sp, ch 2 for first hdc, working in bk lps only, * hdc in ea st to corner sp, (hdc, ch 2, hdc) in corner sp, rep from * around, end with sl st in top of beg ch-2.

Fasten off after rnd 3.

Rnds 4–6: Join cream with sl st in corner sp, rep rnd 2. Fasten off after rnd 6.

Rnds 7 and 8: Join medium terra cotta with sl st in corner sp, rep rnd 2. Fasten off after rnd 8.

Rnds 9–11: Join tan with sl st in corner sp, rep rnd 2.

Rnd 12: Sl st backward into corner sp, ch 1, * sc in ea st to corner, (sc, ch 1, sc) in corner sp, rep from * around, end with sl st in beg ch-1. Fasten off.

THROUGH THE *Seasons*

Celebrate the holidays or mark the changing seasons with a display of your crochet skill. Snowflakes, watermelons, Christmas trees, and jack-o'-lanterns are among the motifs you can choose from to dress your home for any occasion.

Red, White & True

Show your patriotic spirit with this star-spangled afghan.

FINISHED SIZE
Approximately 46" x 62".

MATERIALS
Sportweight acrylic-wool blend (175-yd. ball): 5 each dark country blue, dark country red; 6 cream.

Sizes E and G crochet hooks, or size to obtain gauge.

GAUGE
4 sts and 6 rows in pat = 2" with size G hook.

DIRECTIONS
Solid flag (make 6 ea using colors as foll):

Color A (body)	Color B (box)
Cream	Dk. country red
Dk. country blue	Cream
Dk. country red	Cream

Row 1: With size G hook and A, ch 45, hdc in 3rd ch from hook, (sk next ch, 2 hdc in next ch) 20 times, sk next ch, hdc in last ch, turn.

Rows 2–9: Ch 2 for first hdc, hdc in same st, (sk next st, 2 hdc in next st) 20 times, sk next st, hdc in last st, turn.

Row 10: Ch 2 for first hdc, hdc in same st, (sk next st, 2 hdc in next st) 12 times, drop A and do not carry it across the row, join B, (sk next st, 2 hdc in next st) 8 times, sk next st, hdc in last st, turn.

Row 11: Ch 2 for first hdc, hdc in same st, (sk next st, 2 hdc in next st) 8 times, drop B and do not carry it across the row, using A, (sk next st, 2 hdc in next st) 12 times, sk next st, hdc in last st, turn.

Rows 12–18: Rep rows 10 and 11 alternately. Fasten off after row 18.

Striped flag (make the number shown in parentheses using colors as foll):

Color A (stripes)	Color B (stripes)	Color C (box)
(6) Cream	Dk. country blue	Dk. country red
(12) Cream	Dk. country red	Dk. country blue

Rows 1–3: With size G hook and A, rep rows 1–3 as for solid flag.

Row 4: Join B and carrying A across to end of row by working over it, rep row 2.

Rows 5 and 6: Using B, rep row 2, carrying A loosely up side of block. Drop B at end of row 6.

Row 7: Using A and carrying B across to end of row by working over it, rep row 2.

Rows 8 and 9: Using A, rep row 2, carrying B loosely up side of block. Fasten off A after row 9.

Row 10: Using B, ch 2 for first hdc, hdc in same st, (sk next st, 2 hdc in next st) 12 times, drop B and do not carry it across the row, join C, (sk next st, 2 hdc in next st) 8 times, sk next st, hdc in last st, turn.

Row 11: Using C, ch 2 for first hdc, hdc in same st, (sk next st, 2 hdc in next st) 8 times, drop C and do not carry it across the row, using B, (sk next st, 2 hdc in next st) 12 times, sk next st, hdc in last st, turn.

Row 12: Rep row 10.

Row 13: Using C, ch 2 for first hdc, hdc in same st, (sk next st, 2 hdc in next st) 8 times, drop C and do not carry it across the row, join A and carrying B across to end, (sk next st, 2 hdc in next st) 12 times, sk next st, hdc in last st, turn.

Rows 14 and 15: Using A for stripe and C for box, rep rows 10 and 11, carrying B loosely up side of block. Fasten off A after row 15.

Rows 16–18: Using B for stripe and C for box, rep rows 10 and 11 alternately. Fasten off after row 18.

Star (make 12 dark country blue, 6 cream): With size E hook, ch 4, join with a sl st to form a ring.

Rnd 1: Ch 1, 10 sc in ring, sl st in first sc.

Rnd 2: * Ch 7, sl st in first ch, sc in next ch, hdc in ea of next 2 ch, dc in ea of last 2 ch, sk next sc of ring, sc in next sc, rep from * 4 times more, end with sl st in first sc of ring. Fasten off.

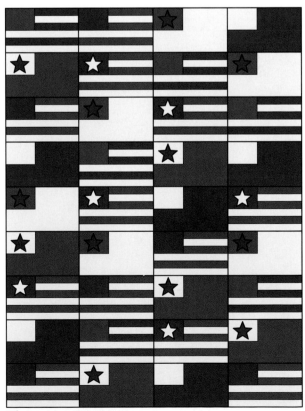

Placement Diagram

Assembly: With right sides facing and referring to placement diagram, whipstitch flag blocks together and stitch stars to flags.

Edging: **Rnd 1:** With right side facing and afghan turned to work across long edge, join dark country blue with sl st in corner, * (sc, ch 1, sc) in corner, work 19 sc across edge of ea flag to next corner of afghan, (sc, ch 1, sc) in corner, [sc in ea st across to last st of next flag, pull up a lp in last st of same flag, pull up a lp in first st of next flag, yo and pull through all lps on hook (sc dec over 2 sts made)] across to next corner of afghan, rep from * around, end with sl st in first sc.

    Rnd 2: Sl st into corner sp, ch 2 for first hdc, (hdc, ch 1, 2 hdc) in same corner, * (hdc in ea of next 4 sts, 2 hdc in next st) across to corner sp, adjusting as necessary to have 207 sts across long edge, (2 hdc, ch 1, 2 hdc) in corner sp, (hdc in ea of next 41 sts, hdc dec over next 2 sts) across to corner sp, adjusting as necessary to have 169 sts across short edge, (2 hdc, ch 1, 2 hdc) in corner sp, rep from * around, end with sl st in top of beg ch-2.

    Rnds 3–5: Sl st into corner sp, ch 2 for first hdc, (hdc, ch 1, 2 hdc) in same corner, * (sk next st, 2 hdc in next st) to corner sp, (2 hdc, ch 1, 2 hdc) in corner sp, rep from * around, end with sl st in top of beg ch-2, turn.

    Rnd 6: Sl st into corner sp, ch 2 for first sc and ch 1, sc in same sp, * sc in ea st to corner sp, (sc, ch 1, sc) in corner sp, rep from * around, end with sl st in first ch of beg ch-2. Fasten off.

For My Valentine

Declare your love for someone special with a throw full of hearts.

FINISHED SIZE
Approximately 66" x 90".

MATERIALS
    Worsted-weight acrylic (240-yd. skein): 2 medium rose, 3 light rose, 4 rose, 12 cream.
    Size F crochet hook, or size to obtain gauge.

GAUGE
    4 sc and 2 rows in pat = 1".

DIRECTIONS
Square (make 16 medium rose, 32 light rose, 45 rose, 49 cream): **Row 1:** Ch 17, hdc in 3rd ch from hook and ea ch across, turn = 16 hdc.

    Row 2: Ch 2 for first hdc, working in ft lps only, * sk next st, hdc in next st, working backward behind prev hdc, hdc in sk st (cross st made), rep from * 6 times more, hdc in last st, turn.

    Row 3: Ch 2 for first hdc, working through both lps, hdc in ea st across, turn.

    Rows 4–9: Rep rows 2 and 3 alternately. Fasten off after row 9.

Heart block assembly: With right sides facing and referring to placement diagram, whipstitch squares together to form 31 heart blocks.

Heart block border: **Rnd 1:** Join cream in any corner, ch 1, * work 32 sc across to next corner, (sc, ch 1, sc) in corner, rep from * around, end with sl st in first sc.

    Rnd 2: Sl st backward into corner sp, ch 2 for first hdc, working in bk lps only, * (cross st over next 2 sts) 17 times, (hdc, ch 1, hdc) in corner sp, rep from * around, end with sl st in top of beg ch-2 = 17 cross sts bet corners.

    Rnd 3: Ch 1, working in bk lps only, * sc in ea st to corner sp, (sc, ch 1, sc) in corner sp, rep from * around, sl st in beg ch-1. Fasten off.

Half-square (make 36): **Row 1:** With cream, ch 3, 2 hdc in 3rd ch from hook, turn = 3 sts.

    Row 2: Ch 2 for first hdc, hdc in same st, hdc in next st, 2 hdc in last st, turn = 5 sts.

    Rows 3–9: Ch 2 for first hdc, hdc in same st, hdc in ea st across to last st, 2 hdc in last st, turn. Fasten off after row 9.

Edge triangle assembly: With right sides facing and referring to placement diagram, whipstitch 2 half-squares to each of 10 cream squares.

Edge triangle border: **Rnd 1:** With right side facing, join cream with sl st in corner of square, ch 1, work 32 sc across to corner, (sc, ch 1, sc) in corner, work 17 sc across half-square, pull up a lp in last st of same half-square, pull up a lp in first st of next half-square, yo and pull through all lps on hook (sc dec over 2 sts made), work 17 sc across half-square to corner, (sc, ch 1, sc) in corner, work 32 sc across to beg corner, sc in same st as beg ch-1, ch 1, sl st in beg ch-1.

Rnd 2: Sl st backward into corner sp, ch 2 for first hdc, working in bk lps only, (cross st over next 2 sts) across to st before corner sp, hdc in next st, (hdc, ch 1, hdc) in corner sp, hdc in next st, (cross st over next 2 sts) 8 times, sk next st, (cross st over next 2 sts) 8 times, hdc in next st, (hdc, ch 1, hdc) in corner sp, (cross st over next 2 sts) 17 times, hdc in beg corner sp, ch 1, sl st in top of beg ch-2.

Rnd 3: Sl st backward into corner sp, ch 1, working in bk lps only, * sc in ea st to corner sp, (sc, ch 1, sc) in corner sp, rep from * around, end with sl st in beg ch-1. Fasten off.

Corner triangle assembly (make 4): With right sides facing and referring to placement diagram, whipstitch 2 half-squares to each of 8 remaining cream squares. With right sides facing and referring to placement diagram, whipstitch 2 triangle pieces together to form corner triangle. Repeat to make 3 more corner triangles.

Corner triangle border: **Rnd 1:** With right side facing and working through both lps, join cream with sl st in center joining bet squares of corner triangle, ch 1, work 34 sc across to corner, (sc, ch 1, sc) in corner, [work 16 sc across half-square, pull up a lp in last st of same half-square, pull up a lp in first st of next half-square, yo and pull through all lps on hook (sc dec over 2 sts made), work 16 sc across to corner, (sc, ch 1, sc) in corner] twice, work 34 sc across to beg ch-1, sl st in beg ch-1.

Rnd 2: Ch 2 for first hdc, working in bk lps only, * (cross st over next 2 sts) to st before corner sp, hdc in next st, (hdc, ch 1, hdc) in corner sp, hdc in next st, rep from * around, end with sl st in top of beg ch-2.

Rnd 3: Ch 1, working in bk lps only, * sc in ea st to corner sp, (sc, ch 1, sc) in corner sp, rep from * around, sl st in beg ch-1. Fasten off.

Assembly: With right sides facing and referring to placement diagram, whipstitch pieces together.

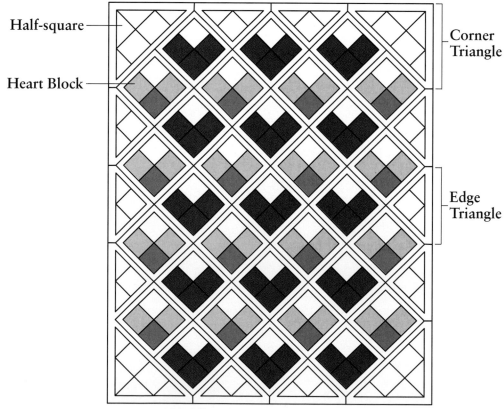

Half-square

Heart Block

Corner Triangle

Edge Triangle

Placement Diagram

Spring Rainbow

*The tiny blocks in this afghan are so easy
to make, you'll have a roomful of
rainbows in no time at all.*

FINISHED SIZE
Approximately 44" x 56".

MATERIALS
Worsted-weight acrylic (240-yd. skein): 6 baby blue; 2 each light purple, aqua; 1 each light yellow, peach, baby pink, mint green.
Size E crochet hook, or size to obtain gauge.

GAUGE
Square = 2¼".

DIRECTIONS
Block (make 215 baby blue; 68 light purple; 48 aqua; 36 ea light yellow, peach, baby pink, mint green): **Row 1:** Ch 12, (hdc, dc) in 3rd ch from hook, * sk next 2 ch, (sc, hdc, dc) in next ch, rep from * once more, sk next 2 ch, sc in last ch, turn.

Rows 2–6: Ch 1, (hdc, dc) in same st, * (sc, hdc, dc) in next sc, rep from * once more, sc in last st, turn. Fasten off after row 6.

Assembly: With right sides facing and referring to photo for color placement, whipstitch blocks together.

115

Nutcracker Sweet

To ensure sweet dreams, crochet this soft
cotton coverlet embellished with tiny
characters from The Nutcracker.

FINISHED SIZE
Approximately 51" x 72".

MATERIALS
Worsted-weight cotton (109-yd. ball): 4 each light yellow, baby pink, mint green, aqua; 5 white; 7 light purple; 11 baby blue.

Sizes E and F crochet hooks, or size to obtain gauge.

Size 3 pearl cotton (16-yd. skein): 4 white (for cross-stitch).

Size 5 pearl cotton (27-yd. skein): 2 each very light peach, medium pink, dark golden brown, pearl gray; 1 each light baby blue, dark steel gray, tan, light pale yellow.

Sizes 6 and 7 steel crochet hooks.

Kreinik's Balger gold braid #32.

GAUGE
With worsted-weight yarn and size F hook: 19 dc and 8 rows = 4".

DIRECTIONS
Seed st block 1 (make 5 ea light yellow, baby blue; 4 ea white, mint green; 3 ea baby pink, light purple, aqua): **Row 1** (right side): With worsted-weight yarn and size F hook, ch 31, sc in 2nd ch from hook and ea ch across, turn = 31 sts.

Row 2: Ch 3 for first dc, (sc in next st, dc in next st) across, turn.

Row 3: Ch 1, (dc in next sc, sc in next dc) across, turn.

Rows 4–26: Rep rows 2 and 3 alternately.

Row 27: Ch 1, sc in ea st across. Fasten off.

Dc block 2 (make 5 ea baby pink, aqua; 4 ea white, mint green; 3 ea light yellow, baby blue, light purple): **Row 1** (right side): With worsted-weight yarn and size F hook, ch 33, dc in 4th ch from hook and ea ch across, turn = 31 sts.

Rows 2–13: Ch 3 for first dc, dc in ea st across, turn. Fasten off.

Assembly: With right sides facing and referring to placement diagram, whipstitch blocks together.

Edging: **Rnd 1:** With right side facing and size E hook, join light purple in any corner, ch 1, * work 26 sc across ea block to corner of afghan, (sc, ch 1, sc) in corner, rep from * around, end with sl st in beg ch-1.

Rnds 2–4: Sl st backward into corner sp, ch 1, working in bk lps only, * sc in ea st to corner sp, (sc, ch 1, sc) in corner sp, rep from * around, end with sl st in beg ch-1.

Rnds 5 and 6: Sl st backward into corner sp, ch 3 for first dc, working through both lps, dc in same sp, * dc in ea st to corner sp, (2 dc, ch 1, 2 dc) in corner sp, rep from * around, end with sl st in top of beg ch-3. Turn after rnd 6.

Rnd 7: Sl st into corner sp, rep rnd 5, turn. Fasten off.

Rnd 8: Join white with sl st in any corner sp, ch 1, * sc in ea st to corner sp, (sc, ch 1, sc) in corner sp, rep from * around, end with sl st in beg ch-1, turn.

Rnd 9: Sl st into corner sp, rep rnd 8, turn. Fasten off.

Rnd 10: Join baby blue with sl st in any corner sp, ch 3 for first dc, dc in same sp, * dc in ea st to corner sp, (2 dc, ch 1, 2 dc) in corner sp, rep from * around, end with sl st in top of beg ch-3, sl st backward into corner sp.

Rnds 11–22: Ch 1, working in bk lps only, * sc in ea st to corner sp, (sc, ch 1, sc) in corner sp, rep from * around, end with sl st in beg ch-1.

Rnd 23: Ch 3 for first dc, working through both lps, * dc in ea st to corner sp, (dc, ch 1, dc) in corner sp, rep from * around, end with sl st in top of beg ch-3. Fasten off.

Cross-stitch: Centering design on blue band of edging (rnds 11–22) and using 1 length of white

Placement Diagram

size 3 pearl cotton, cross-stitch "The Nutcracker" on each edge of afghan according to chart (see photo).

Sugar plum fairy (make 4): Use size 7 steel crochet hook with specified colors of pearl cotton thread.
Head: Rnd 1: With very light peach pearl cotton, ch 2, 8 sc in 2nd ch from hook, sl st in first sc.

Note: Work in a spiral. Use a safety pin to mark beg of ea rnd.

Rnd 2: Work 2 sc in ea st around = 16 sts.

Rnd 3: (Sc in next st, 2 sc in next st) around = 24 sts.

Rnd 4: Work (2 sc in next st, sc in ea of next 2 sts) around = 32 sts, sl st in first st of rnd. Fasten off.

Arms and neck: Row 1: With very light peach pearl cotton, ch 31, sc in 2nd ch from hook and ea ch across, turn = 31 sts.

Row 2: Ch 1, sc in ea of next 13 sts, dc in ea of next 3 sts (for neck), sc in ea of rem 14 sts. Fasten off.

Whipstitch head to 3 dc sts at neck.

Note: With right side facing, turn arms piece upside down and beg working dress in unworked side of base ch of arms.

Dress: Row 1: Join medium pink pearl cotton with sl st in 12th st of arms piece, ch 1, sc in ea of next 8 sts, turn = 9 sts.

Row 2: Ch 1, sc in ea of next 8 sts, turn.

Row 3: Ch 1, pull up a lp in ea of next 2 sts, yo and pull through all 3 lps on hook (sc dec over 2 sts made), sc in ea of next 3 sts, sc dec over next 2 sts, sc in last st, turn = 7 sts.

Row 4: Ch 1, sc in ea of next 6 sts, turn.

Row 5: Ch 1, sc dec over next 2 sts, sc in next st, sc dec over next 2 sts, sc in last st, turn = 5 sts.

Row 6: Ch 1, sc in ea of next 4 sts, turn.

Row 7: Ch 2 for first hdc, hdc in same st, hdc in ea of next 3 sts, 2 hdc in last st, turn = 7 sts.

Row 8: Ch 3 for first dc, (2 dc, ch 1, 3 dc) in same st, * sk next 2 sts, (3 dc, ch 1, 3 dc) in next st (shell made), rep from * once more, turn.

Row 9: Ch 4 for first dc and ch 1, dc in same st, * ch 1, dc in next ch-1 sp, ch 1 **, sk 1 st, dc in next st, ch 1, dc bet shells, ch 1, sk 1 st, dc in next st, rep from * twice more, end last rep at **, (dc, ch 1, dc) in last st, turn.

Row 10: (Ch 3, sc in next ch-1 sp) 12 times, ch

3, sl st in last st = 13 lps. Fasten off.

Leg: With right side facing, join very light peach pearl cotton with sl st in 6th lp of dress, ch 13, sc in 2nd ch from hook, sc in ea of next 2 ch, hdc in ea of next 3 ch, sc in next ch, hdc in ea of next 2 ch, dc in ea of next 3 ch, sl st in same lp on dress as beg sl st. Fasten off.

With right side facing, sk 1 lp of dress and make 2nd leg as est.

Slipper: Join medium pink pearl cotton with sl st in st at end of leg, ch 4 for first tr, keeping last lp of ea st on hook, work 2 tr in same st, yo and pull through all lps on hook, ch 1. Fasten off.

Rep to work a slipper in 2nd leg.

Hair: Cut 17 (6") strands of dark golden brown pearl cotton. Beginning in 7th stitch from neck, knot 1 (6") strand in each of next 16 stitches of head. For bangs, cut 5 (1") strands of dark golden brown pearl cotton. Knot 1 strand in each of center 5 stitches of head in front of hair. Cut 1 (11") strand of medium pink pearl cotton and tie in a bow around hair.

Soldier (make 1): Use size 7 steel crochet hook with specified colors of pearl cotton thread. **Face: Row 1:** With very light peach pearl cotton, ch 2, 4 sc in 2nd ch from hook, turn.

Row 2: Ch 1, 2 sc in ea of next 4 sts, turn.

Row 3: Ch 1, sc in same st, (sc in next st, 2 sc in next st) across, turn.

Row 4: Ch 1, (sc in ea of next 2 sts, 2 sc in next st) across. Fasten off.

Note: With right side facing, turn face piece upside down and beg working hat across straight edge of face.

Hat: Row 1: Join light baby blue pearl cotton with sl st in st at edge of face, ch 1, work 8 sc across edge of face, turn.

Row 2: Ch 1, sc in ea of next 8 sts, turn.

Row 3: Ch 2 for first hdc, hdc in same st, hdc in ea of next 7 sts, 2 hdc in last st, turn.

Rows 4 and 5: Ch 2 for first hdc, hdc in ea st across, turn.

Row 6: Ch 1, sc in same st, sc in ea st across to last st, 2 sc in last st. Fasten off.

Jacket: Row 1 (right side): (*Note:* Jacket is worked from neck edge down.) With light baby blue pearl cotton, ch 15, sc in 2nd ch from hook and ea ch across, turn.

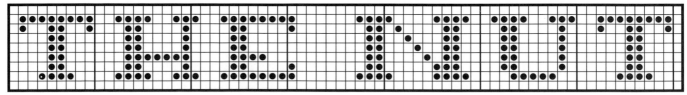

Cross-stitch Chart

Row 2: Ch 1, sc in ea of next 14 sts, turn.

Rows 3 and 4: Ch 2 for first hdc, hdc in ea of next 14 sts, turn.

First sleeve (short rows): **Row 1:** Ch 2 for first hdc, hdc in ea of next 3 sts, turn.

Rows 2–5: Ch 2 for first hdc, hdc in ea of next 3 sts, turn.

Row 6: Ch 1, sc in ea of next 3 sts. Fasten off.

Body (short rows): **Row 1:** With right side facing, join light baby blue pearl cotton with sl st in unworked row-4 st after first sleeve, ch 2 for first hdc, hdc in same st, hdc in ea of next 5 sts, 2 hdc in next st, turn.

Rows 2–7: Ch 2 for first hdc, hdc in ea of next 8 sts, turn.

Row 8: Ch 1, sc in same st, sc in ea of next 7 sts, 2 sc in last st. Fasten off.

2nd sleeve (short rows): **Row 1:** With right side facing, join light baby blue pearl cotton with sl st in unworked row-4 st after jacket body, rep rows 1–6 as for first sleeve. Fasten off. Do not turn.

First pants leg: Row 1: With right side facing, join pearl gray pearl cotton with sl st in 2nd st from edge on last row of jacket, ch 1, working in bk lps only, sc in ea of next 4 sts, turn.

Rows 2–11: Ch 1, working through both lps, sc in ea of next 4 sts, turn. Fasten off after row 11.

2nd pants leg: Rows 1–11: With right side facing, join pearl gray pearl cotton with sl st in same st as last st of first pants leg, rep rows 1–11 as for first pants leg.

Whipstitch head to center top of jacket. Referring to photo, add gold braid trim to soldier.

Large mouse (make 1): Use size 6 steel crochet hook and pearl gray pearl cotton thread. **Ear** (make 2): Rep rnds 1–4 as for sugar plum fairy head. Fasten off.

Head: Rnds 1–4: Rep rnds 1–4 as for sugar plum fairy head. Do not sl st or fasten off after rnd 4.

Rnd 5: (Sc in ea of next 3 sts, 2 sc in next st) 8 times = 40 sts.

Rnd 6: Sc in ea of next 2 sts, (2 sc in next st, sc in ea of next 4 sts) 7 times, 2 sc in next st, sc in ea of next 2 sts, sl st in next st = 48 sts. Fasten off.

Body: Rnds 1–6: Rep rnds 1–6 as for mouse head. Do not sl st or fasten off after rnd 6.

Rnd 7: (Sc in ea of next 5 sts, 2 sc in next st) 8 times = 56 sts.

Rnd 8: Sc in ea of next 3 sts, (2 sc in next st, sc in ea of next 6 sts) 7 times, sc in ea of next 4 sts.

Rnd 9: Sc in ea st around.

Rnd 10: Sc in ea st around, sl st in next st.

Tail: Ch 31, sc in 2nd ch from hook and ea ch across, sl st in next sc on body. Fasten off.

Whipstitch mouse pieces together.

Small mouse (make 1): With size 7 steel crochet hook and dark steel gray pearl cotton thread, work as for large mouse.

Teddy bear (make 1): Use size 6 steel crochet hook and tan pearl cotton thread. **Head:** Rep rnds 1–6 as for large mouse head.

Body: Rnd 1: Ch 6, 2 sc in 2nd ch from hook, sc in ea of next 3 ch, 3 sc in next ch, working across opposite side of base ch, sc in ea of next 3 sts, sc in same ch as beg, sl st in first sc = 12 sts.

Rnd 2: Ch 1, sc in same st, sc in ea of next 5 sts, 3 sc in next st, sc in ea of next 5 sts, sc in same st as beg ch-1, sl st in beg ch-1 = 16 sts.

Rnd 3: Ch 1, * 2 sc in next st, sc in ea of next 5 sts, 2 sc in next st **, sc in next st, rep from * to **, sl st in beg ch-1 = 20 sts.

Rnd 4: Ch 1, * 2 sc in ea of next 2 sts, sc in ea

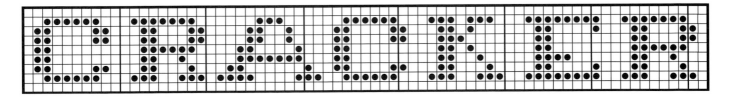

of next 5 sts, 2 sc in ea of next 2 sts **, sc in next st, rep from * to **, sl st in beg ch-1 = 28 sts.

Rnd 5: Ch 1, * 2 sc in ea of next 3 sts, sc in ea of next 7 sts, 2 sc in ea of next 3 sts **, sc in next st, rep from * to **, sl st in beg ch-1 = 40 sts.

Rnd 6: Ch 1, sc in ea of next 2 sts, * 2 sc in next st, sc in ea of next 13 sts, 2 sc in next st **, sc in ea of next 5 sts, rep from * to **, sc in ea of next 2 sts, sl st in beg ch-1 = 44 sts. Fasten off.

Whipstitch head to body.

Ears: Row 1: Join thread with sl st in 16th st from neck, 3 sc in next st, sl st in ea of next 2 sts of head, turn.

Row 2: Sc in next sc, 3 sc in next sc, sc in next sc, sl st in ea of next 2 sts of head, turn.

Row 3: Sc in next sc, 3 sc in ea of next 3 sc, sc in next sc, sl st in next st of head. Fasten off.

Sk 8 sts across top of head, join thread with sl st in next st, rep rows 1–3 to make 2nd ear.

Arms and legs (make 4): **Rnd 1:** Ch 9, sc in 2nd ch from hook and ea of next 6 ch, 3 sc in last ch, working across opposite side of base ch, sc in ea of next 6 ch, 2 sc in same ch as beg, sl st in first sc.

Note: Work in a spiral. Use a safety pin to mark the beg of ea rnd.

Rnd 2: Sc in ea of next 8 sts, 3 sc in next st, sc in ea of next 8 sts, 3 sc in next st.

Rnd 3: (Sc in ea of next 8 sts, 2 sc in next st, sc in next st, 2 sc in next st) twice, sl st in next st. Fasten off.

Whipstitch arms and legs to body.

Star (make 5): **Rnd 1:** With size 7 hook and light pale yellow pearl cotton, ch 2, 5 sc in 2nd ch from hook, sl st in first sc.

Rnd 2: Ch 3 for first dc, 2 dc in same st, 3 dc in ea of next 4 sts, sl st in top of beg ch-3.

Rnd 3: Ch 1, sc in same st, * ch 10, sl st in 2nd ch from hook, sc in next ch, hdc in ea of next 2 ch, dc in ea of next 3 ch, tr in ea of next 2 ch, tr in side of sc at base of ch-10, sk 2 dc on star, sc in next dc, rep from * 4 times more, end with sl st in first sc. Fasten off.

Finishing: Referring to photo for positioning, stitch figures and stars to blocks.

Christmas Wishes

Cross-stitch heartfelt season's greetings on an afghan-stitch background to craft this holiday wish for your home.

FINISHED SIZE
Approximately 47" x 68".

MATERIALS
Worsted-weight acrylic-wool blend (200-yd. skein): 18 beige heather.
Size H afghan hook, or size to obtain gauge.
Sportweight acrylic (175-yd. ball): 1 holly green (for cross-stitch).
Worsted-weight acrylic (110-yd. skein): 1 burgundy (for cross-stitch).
Size H crochet hook.

GAUGE
7 sts and 6 rows = 2" in afghan st.

DIRECTIONS
Note: See page 141 for afghan st directions.

Block (make 108): With afghan hook and beige heather, ch 16, work 15 rows afghan st. Sl st in ea vertical bar across. Do not fasten off.

Border: Sc in same st, * sc in ea st to next corner, (sc, ch 1, sc) in corner st, rep from * around, sl st in first sc. Fasten off.

Cross-stitch: Centering design on block and using 1 strand of holly green yarn, cross-stitch 1 heart on each of 5 blocks. Centering each letter on block and using 1 strand of burgundy yarn, refer to alphabet chart to cross-stitch letters to spell Peace, Merry Christmas, Love, Noel, and Joy.

Assembly: With right sides facing and referring to placement diagram, whipstitch blocks together through back loops only.

Edging: With crochet hook and right side facing, join beige heather with sl st in st before corner sp, ch 1, working in crab st (reverse sc) from left to right (instead of right to left), * sc in ea st across to corner sp, (sc, ch 1, sc) in corner sp, rep from * around, end with sl st in beg ch-1. Fasten off.

Placement Diagram

Color Key

Brunswick Yarns

○ Fore-n'-Aft (1 strand)
60043 Holly Green

△ Pearl (1 strand)
5924 Burgundy

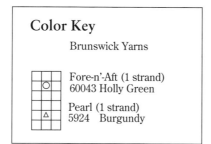

Heart Cross-stitch Chart

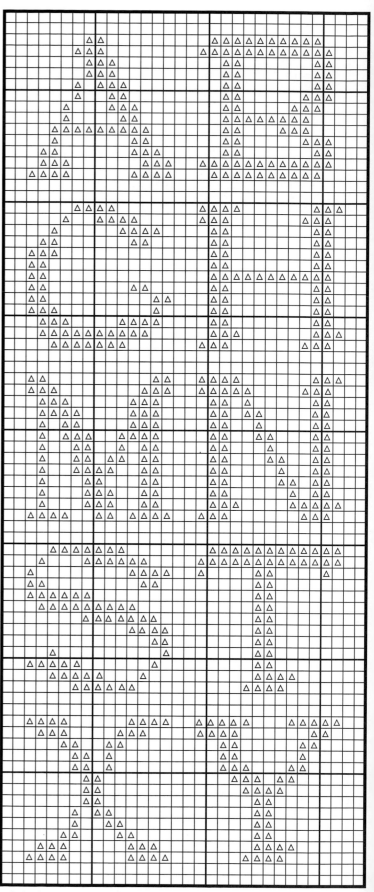

Alphabet Cross-stitch Chart

122

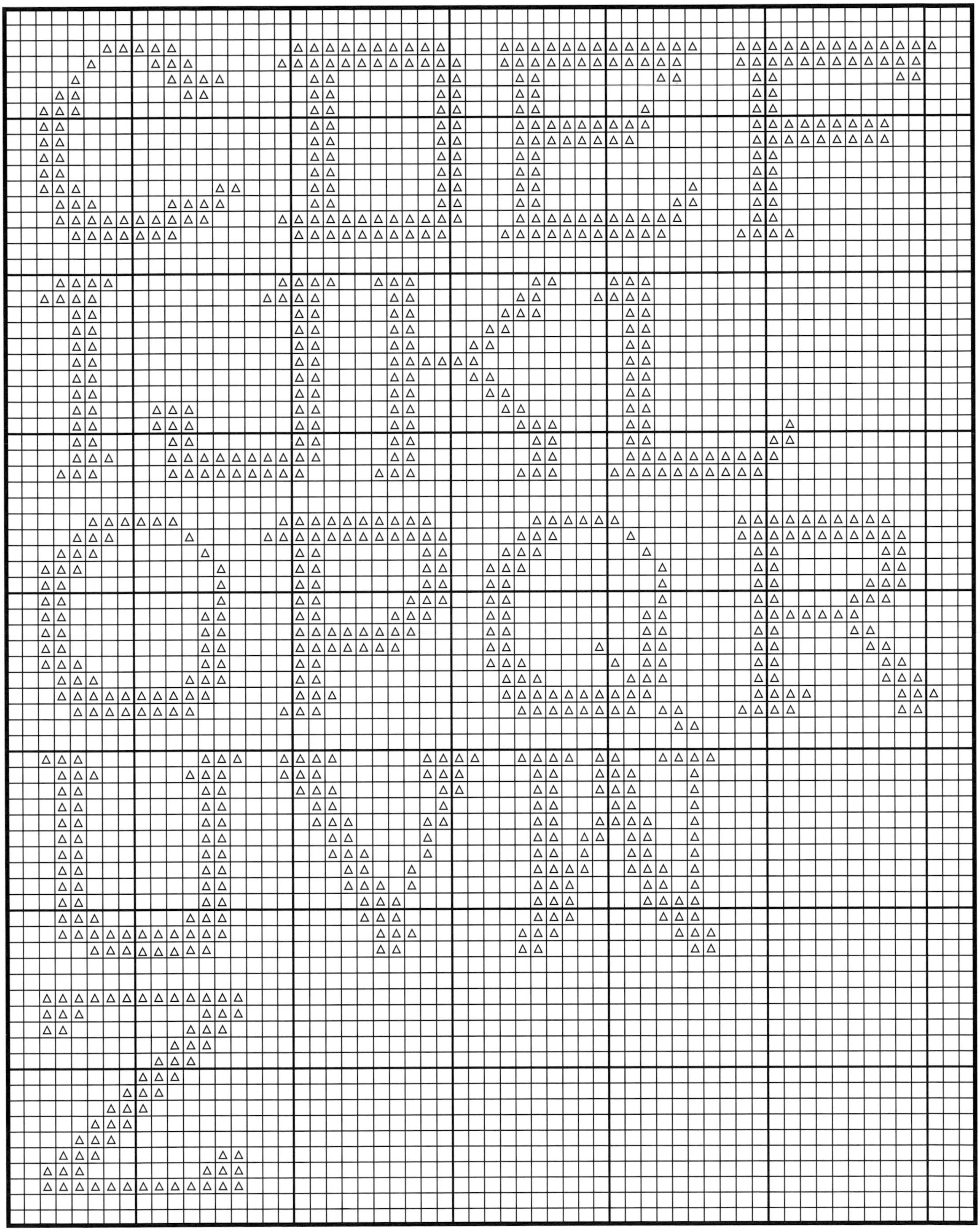

Snowflakes

Chase away a winter chill with this wool throw featuring soft blue snowflakes.

FINISHED SIZE
Approximately 46" square.

MATERIALS
Fingering-weight wool (202-yd. skein): 7 light blue, 9 cream.

Size E crochet hook, or size to obtain gauge.

GAUGE
5 hdc and 3 rows = 1".

DIRECTIONS
Note: For ea hdc, pull up ½" lps.

Large block (make 5 light blue, 24 cream): **Row 1:** Ch 32, hdc in 3rd ch from hook and ea ch across, turn = 31 sts.

Rows 2–17: Ch 2 for first hdc, (hdc in bk lp only of next st, hdc in ft lp only of next st) 14 times, hdc in bk lp only of next st, hdc in last st, turn.

Row 18: Ch 2 for first hdc, hdc in ea st across. Fasten off.

Small solid block (make 40): **Row 1:** With cream, ch 10, sc in 2nd ch from hook and ea ch across, turn = 10 sts.

Rows 2–11: Ch 1, sc in ea st across, turn. Fasten off after row 11.

Small two-color block (make 80): **Row 1:** With cream, ch 2, 2 sc in 2nd ch from hook, turn.

Row 2: Ch 1, sc in same st, sc in next st, 2 sc in last st, turn.

Rows 3–8: Ch 1, sc in same st, sc in ea st across to last st, 2 sc in last st, turn. Fasten off after row 8.

Row 9: Join light blue with sl st in last st of prev row, ch 1, sc in ea of next 13 sts, pull up a lp in ea of next 3 sts, yo and pull through all 4 lps on hook (sc dec over 3 sts made), turn.

Rows 10–15: Ch 1, sc in ea st across to last 3 sts, sc dec over last 3 sts, turn.

Row 16: Ch 1, sc dec over last 2 sts. Fasten off.

Rectangle (make 20): **Row 1:** With light blue, ch 10, sc in 2nd ch from hook and ea ch across, turn = 10 sts.

Rows 2–33: Ch 1, sc in ea st across, turn. Fasten off after row 33.

Assembly: With right sides facing and referring to placement diagram, whipstitch pieces together.

Edging: **Rnd 1:** With right side facing, join light blue with sl st in corner, ch 2 for first hdc, * hdc across to corner (inc as necessary to have an odd number of sts across edge), (hdc, ch 1, hdc) in corner, rep from * around, end with sl st in top of beg ch-2, turn.

Rnd 2: Ch 2 for first hdc, * hdc in bk lp only of next st, (hdc in ft lp only of next st, hdc in bk lp only of next st) to corner sp, (hdc, ch 1, hdc) in corner sp, rep from * around, end with sl st in top of beg ch-2, turn.

Rnd 3: Sl st into corner sp, ch 2 for first hdc, * hdc in ft lp only of next st, (hdc in bk lp only of next st, hdc in ft lp only of next st) to corner sp, (hdc, ch 2, hdc) in corner sp, rep from * around, end with sl st in top of beg ch-2, turn.

Rnd 4: Sl st into corner sp, ch 2 for first hdc, * sc in ea of next 8 sts, pull up a lp in ea of next 2 sts, yo and pull through all 3 lps on hook (sc dec over 2 sts made), rep from * to corner sp, (hdc, ch 1, hdc) in corner sp, rep from * around, end with sl st in top of beg ch-2, turn.

Rnds 5–7: Sl st into corner sp, ch 2, * sc in ea st to corner sp, (hdc, ch 1, hdc) in corner sp, rep from * around, end with sl st in top of beg ch-2, turn.

Rnds 8 and 9: Rep rnds 2 and 3. Do not turn after rnd 9.

Rnd 10: Ch 1, working in bk lps only, * sc in ea st to corner sp, (sc, ch 1, sc) in corner sp, rep from * around, end with sl st in first sc. Fasten off.

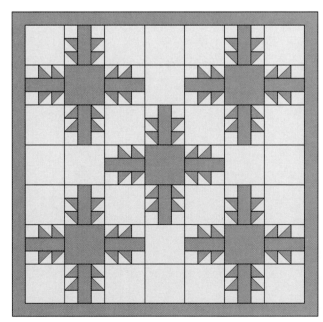

Placement Diagram

Autumn Flight

*Use a heavy cotton yarn in the colors of fall to
make this throw in the classic Flying Geese
quilt pattern.*

FINISHED SIZE
Approximately 60" x 64".

MATERIALS
Worsted-weight mercerized cotton (93-yd.
skein): 6 gold; 7 each rust, brown; 27 natural.
Size G crochet hook, or size to obtain gauge.

GAUGE
8 hdc and 5 rows = 2".

DIRECTIONS
Triangle (make 8 rust, 34 gold, 36 brown): **Row 1:**
Ch 22, hdc in 3rd ch from hook and ea ch across,
turn = 21 hdc.

Row 2: Ch 2, yo and pull up a lp in same st as
tch, yo and pull up a lp in next st, yo and pull
through all lps on hook (hdc dec over same st as
tch and next st made), yo and pull up a lp in ea of
next 2 sts, yo and pull through all lps on hook
(hdc dec over 2 sts made), hdc in ea of next 13 sts,
(hdc dec over next 2 sts) twice, turn.

Row 3: Ch 2, hdc dec over same st as tch and
next st, hdc in ea of next 13 sts, hdc dec over last 2
sts, turn.

Row 4: Ch 2, hdc dec over same st as tch and
next st, hdc dec over next 2 sts, hdc in ea of next 7
sts, (hdc dec over next 2 sts) twice, turn.

Row 5: Ch 2, hdc dec over same st as tch and
next st, hdc in ea of next 7 sts, hdc dec over last 2
sts, turn.

Row 6: Ch 2, hdc dec over same st as tch and
next st, hdc dec over next 2 sts, hdc in next st,
(hdc dec over next 2 sts) twice, turn.

Row 7: Ch 2, hdc dec over same st as tch and
next st, hdc in next st, hdc dec over last 2 sts, turn.

Row 8: Ch 2, hdc dec over same st as tch and ea
of next 2 sts, turn.

Border: Ch 1, sc in same st, 2 sc in side of ea
row to next point of triangle, (sc, ch 1, sc) in st at
point, sc in ea st to next point, (sc, ch 1, sc) in st at
point, 2 sc in side of ea row to beg point, sc in
same st as beg, ch 1, sl st in first sc. Fasten off.

Narrow strip (make 5): **Row 1:** With rust, ch 11,
hdc in 3rd ch from hook and ea ch across, turn =
10 hdc.

Rows 2–136: Ch 2 for first hdc, hdc in ea st
across, turn. Fasten off after row 136.

Wide strip (make 6): **Row 1:** With natural, ch 27,
hdc in 3rd ch from hook and ea ch across, turn =
26 hdc.

Rows 2–136: Ch 2 for first hdc, hdc in ea st
across, turn. Fasten off after row 136.

Assembly: With right sides facing and beginning
with a wide strip, whipstitch strips together, alternating wide and narrow strips. Referring to photo,
stitch 13 triangles to each wide strip, using colors
as desired and alternating direction of triangles on
adjacent strips.

Edging: **Rnd 1:** With right side facing, join rust
with sl st in corner, * (sc, ch 1, sc) in corner, sc in
ea st to next corner, rep from * around, end with sl
st in first sc.

Rnd 2: Sl st into corner sp, ch 2 for first hdc,
* hdc in ea st to next corner sp, (hdc, ch 1, hdc) in
corner sp, rep from * around, end with sl st in top
of beg ch-2.

Rnds 3 and 4: Rep rnd 2. Fasten off after rnd 4.

Rnds 5–13: Join natural with sl st in corner sp,
rep rnd 2. Fasten off after rnd 13.

Rnds 14–16: Join gold with sl st in corner sp,
rep rnd 2. Fasten off after rnd 16.

Rnds 17 and 18: Join natural with sl st in corner
sp, rep rnd 2. Fasten off after rnd 18.

Rnds 19–21: Join brown with sl st in corner sp,
rep rnd 2. Fasten off after rnd 21.

Deck the Halls

Get ready for the holidays with this afghan boasting Christmas trees and brightly colored packages.

FINISHED SIZE
Approximately 42" x 60".

MATERIALS
Sportweight acrylic (175-yd. ball): 15 cream, 4 dark teal, 1 brown.

Sizes F and G and crochet hooks, or size to obtain gauge.

Paternayan Persian wool (8-yd. skein): 1 each Autumn Yellow #727, Bittersweet #835, Medium American Beauty #903, Dark American Beauty #901, Medium Plum #323, Dark Plum #321, Medium Grape #312, Dark Grape #311, Federal Blue #503, Medium Turquoise #576, Dark Turquoise #575 (for packages).

Size 1 steel crochet hook.

Size 5 pearl cotton (27-yd. skein): 1 each light violet, medium garnet, dark antique blue, light coral, very dark lavender, ecru (for bows).

GAUGE
4 sc and 5 rows = 1" with size G hook.

DIRECTIONS
Block (make 40): **Row 1** (wrong side): With size G hook and cream, ch 34, sc in 2nd ch from hook and ea ch across, turn = 33 sc.

Row 2: Ch 1, sc in ea st across, turn.

Rows 3–8: Ch 1, sc in ea of next 14 sts, join brown and carry cream across by working over it, sc in ea of next 5 sts, drop brown and do not carry it across, using cream, sc in ea of last 14 sts, turn. Fasten off brown after row 8.

Note: For rows 9–29, carry cream across by working over it. Do not carry dark teal across.

Row 9: Ch 1, sc in ea of next 6 sts, join dark teal and carry cream across by working over it, sc in ea of next 21 sts, drop dark teal and do not carry it across, using cream, sc in ea of last 6 sts, turn.

Cont in sc using colors as specified below.

Rows 10–13: 7 sts cream, 19 sts dark teal, 7 sts cream.

Rows 14 and 15: 8 sts cream, 17 sts dark teal, 8 sts cream.

Rows 16 and 17: 9 sts cream, 15 sts dark teal, 9 sts cream.

Rows 18 and 19: 10 sts cream, 13 sts dark teal, 10 sts cream.

Rows 20 and 21: 11 sts cream, 11 sts dark teal, 11 sts cream.

Rows 22 and 23: 12 sts cream, 9 sts dark teal, 12 sts cream.

Rows 24 and 25: 13 sts cream, 7 sts dark teal, 13 sts cream.

Rows 26 and 27: 14 sts cream, 5 sts dark teal, 14 sts cream.

Row 28: 15 sts cream, 3 sts dark teal, 15 sts cream.

Row 29: 16 sts cream, 1 st dark teal, 16 sts cream. Fasten off dark teal.

Rows 30 and 31: Using cream, ch 1, sc in ea st across, turn.

Border: Rnd 1: With right side facing and size F hook, ch 1, * sc in ea st to corner of block, (sc, ch 1, sc) in corner, rep from * around, end with sl st in beg ch-1.

Rnd 2: Sl st backward into corner sp, ch 2 for first hdc, ch 1, hdc in same corner, * hdc in ea st to corner sp, (hdc, ch 1, hdc) in corner sp, rep from * around, end with sl st in top of beg ch-2, turn.

Rnd 3: Sl st into corner sp, ch 1, * sc in ea st to corner sp, (sc, ch 1, sc) in corner sp, rep from * around, end with sl st in beg ch-1. Fasten off.

Assembly: Afghan is 5 blocks wide and 8 blocks long. With right sides facing, whipstitch blocks together through back loops only.

Edging: **Rnd 1:** With right side facing and size F hook, join cream with sl st in any corner, ch 1, * sc in ea st to next corner, (sc, ch 1, sc) in corner, rep from * around, end with sl st in beg ch-1.

Rnd 2: * Ch 3, 3 dc in same st, sk next 3 sts, sl st in next st, rep from * around, end with sl st in same st as beg ch-3. Fasten off.

Packages: Using 1 strand of Paternayan Persian wool and size #1 hook, make packages as desired.

Large package: Row 1: Ch 11, sc in 2nd ch from hook and ea ch across, turn = 11 sts.

Rows 2–11: Ch 1, sc in ea st across, turn. Fasten off after row 11.

Medium package: Work as for rows 1–7 of large package. Fasten off.

Small package: Row 1: Ch 7, sc in 2nd ch from hook and ea ch across, turn = 7 sts.

Rows 2–7: Ch 1, sc in ea st across, turn. Fasten off after row 7.

Bows: Thread a needle with 1 (7") length of pearl cotton and stitch through top center of package from right side; then stitch through bottom center of package from wrong side, leaving thread tails on right side of package. Tie tails together in a bow at top of package. Repeat to make a bow on each package.

Finishing: Stitch packages to Christmas tree blocks as desired (see photo).

Slices of Summer

Inspire thoughts of summer year-round with these blocks of rich red watermelon wedges.

FINISHED SIZE
Approximately 48" x 65".

MATERIALS
Sportweight acrylic (175-yd. ball): 5 green, 6 red, 11 white.
Size E crochet hook, or size to obtain gauge.
Size 3 pearl cotton (16-yd. skein): 2 black.

GAUGE
9 dc and 5 rows = 2".

DIRECTIONS
Block (make 35): **Row 1:** With red, ch 3, 2 dc in 3rd ch from hook, turn.

Row 2: Ch 3 for first dc, 2 dc in same st, dc in next st, 3 dc in next st, turn = 7 sts.

Rows 3–12: Ch 3 for first dc, 2 dc in same st, dc in ea st to last st, 3 dc in last st, turn = inc 4 sts ea row; 47 sts after row 12. Fasten off.

Rows 13–24: Join white with sl st in last st of row 12, ch 2, keeping last lp of ea st on hook, dc in ea of next 2 sts, yo and pull through all lps on hook (dc dec over 2 sts made), dc in ea st across to last 3 sts, dc dec over last 3 sts, turn = dec 4 sts ea row.

Border: Ch 3 for first dc, dc in 3rd ch from hook, * 2 dc in side of ea row to corner, (2 dc, ch 1, 2 dc) in corner, rep from * around, end with 2 dc in beg corner, ch 1, sl st in top of beg ch-3 = 24 sts bet corner grps. Fasten off.

Partial border rows (white): *Note:* Partial border rows are worked across 2 edges of block only.
Row 1: With wrong side facing and block turned to work across white half, join white with sl st in corner sp above red/white seam, ch 3 for first dc, 2 dc in same sp, dc in ea st to next corner sp, (2 dc,

ch 1, 2 dc) in corner sp, dc in ea st to next corner sp, 3 dc in corner sp, turn.

Row 2: Ch 3 for first dc, dc in 3rd ch from hook, dc in ea st to next corner sp, 6 dc in corner sp, dc in ea st to next corner sp, 3 dc in corner st. Fasten off.

Partial border rows (green): With wrong side facing and block turned to work across red half, join green in corner and rep rows 1 and 2 above, except sl st in top of white corner st at end of ea row.

Embroidery: With black, make several lazy daisy stitches on each watermelon as desired for seeds (see photo).

Assembly: Afghan is 5 blocks wide and 7 blocks long. With right sides facing and referring to photo, whipstitch blocks together.

Edging: **Rnd 1:** Join white with sl st in 4th dc of any corner, ch 2 for first hdc, hdc in same st, * hdc in ea st to next corner st, (2 hdc, ch 1, 2 hdc) in corner st, rep from * around, end with sl st in top of beg ch-2.

Rnd 2: Ch 3 for first dc, dc in same st, * dc in ea st to st before corner sp, 2 dc in next st, ch 1, sk corner sp, 2 dc in next st, rep from * around, end with sl st in top of beg ch-3. Fasten off.

Rnds 3–5: Join green with sl st in first dc after any corner sp, rep rnd 2. Fasten off after rnd 5.

Rnd 6: Join red with sl st in first dc after any corner sp, rep rnd 2.

Rnd 7: Ch 1, working in crab st (reverse sc) from left to right (instead of right to left), sc in ea dc and sp around, sl st in beg ch-1. Fasten off.

Pumpkin Trio

Halloween is the time to show off this spooky treat with its grinning jack-o'-lanterns and flapping bats.

FINISHED SIZE
Approximately 44" x 58".

MATERIALS
Worsted-weight wool (138-yd. skein): 1 each dark country blue, brown; 3 dark country green; 8 medium country green.

Sportweight wool (123-yd. ball): 2 medium orange, 6 light orange.

Worsted-weight wool (260-yd. skein): 3 blue.

Worsted-weight wool (137-yd. skein): 1 black.

Sizes D and G crochet hooks, or size to obtain gauge.

GAUGE
4 cl and 6 rows = 2" with size G hook.

DIRECTIONS
Large solid block (make 10 dark country blue, 11 medium orange, 12 dark country green, 24 light orange, 36 blue, 39 medium country green): **Row 1** (wrong side): With size G hook, ch 18, sc in 2nd ch from hook, * pull up a lp in same ch as prev st, pull up a lp in ea of next 2 ch, yo and pull through all lps on hook (cl made), ch 1, rep from * across, end with sc in same st as last leg of last cl, turn = 8 cl.

Rows 2–14: Ch 1, sc in same st, * cl as est over same st as prev st and next 2 sts, ch 1, rep from * across, end with sc in same st as last leg of last cl, turn. Fasten off after row 14.

Large two-color block (make the number shown in parentheses using colors as foll): *Note:* To change colors, work last yo of last st in prev color with both colors held tog as 1.

	Main color (mc)	Contrasting color (cc)
A (2)	Blue	Lt. orange
B (2)	Lt. orange	Blue
C (2)	Med. orange	Blue
D (1)	Lt. orange	Med. orange
E (2)	Med. country green	Lt. orange
F (1)	Lt. orange	Med. country green
G (1)	Med. country green	Med. orange

Row 1 (wrong side): With size G hook and mc, ch 18, sc in 2nd ch from hook, * pull up a lp in same ch as prev st, pull up a lp in ea of next 2 ch, yo and pull through all lps on hook (cl made), ch 1, rep from * across, except work last yo of last cl with mc and cc held tog as 1, drop mc, using cc, ch 1, sc in same st as last leg of last cl, turn.

Row 2: Ch 1, sc in same st, * cl as est over same st as prev st and next 2 sts **, ch 1, rep from * to ** to make another cl, except work last yo with cc and mc held tog as 1, drop cc, using mc, ch 1, (cl, ch 1) 6 times, sc in same st as last leg of last cl, turn = 6 cl with mc and 2 cl with cc.

Row 3: Ch 1, sc in same st, (cl, ch 1) 5 times, cl as est over same st as prev st and next 2 sts, except work last yo with mc and cc held tog as 1, drop mc, using cc, (ch 1, cl) twice, ch 1, sc in same st as last leg of last cl, turn = 6 cl with mc and 2 cl with cc.

Row 4: Ch 1, sc in same st, (cl, ch 1) twice, cl as est over same st as prev st and next 2 sts, except work last yo with cc and mc held tog as 1, drop cc, using mc, (ch 1, cl) 5 times, ch 1, sc in same st as last leg of last cl, turn = 5 cl with mc and 3 cl with cc.

Rows 5–14: Cont as est working 1 more cl in cc and 1 fewer cl in mc every other row = 8 cl with cc after row 14. Fasten off.

Large triangle (make 25 black, 3 brown): **Row 1:** With size D hook, ch 2, sc in 2nd ch from hook, turn.

Row 2: Ch 1, sc in same st, sc in next st, 2 sc in next st, turn.

Rows 3–7: Ch 1, sc in same st, sc in ea st across to last st, 2 sc in last st, turn.

Row 8: Ch 1, sc in ea st across, turn = 13 sts.

Row 9: Ch 1, sc in same st, sc in ea st across to last st, 2 sc in last st, turn.

Row 10: Rep row 8.

Row 11: Ch 1, sc in same st, sc in ea st across to last st, 2 sc in last st, turn.

Row 12: Rep row 8 = 17 sts. Fasten off.

Placement Diagram

Small triangle (make 8): **Rows 1–8:** With size D hook and black, rep rows 1–8 as for large triangle. Fasten off after row 8.

Small block (make 11 black, 3 brown): **Row 1:** With size D hook, ch 10, sc in 2nd ch from hook and ea ch across, turn.

   Rows 2–9: Ch 1, sc in ea st across, turn. Fasten off after row 9.

Assembly: With right sides facing and referring to placement diagram, whipstitch large solid blocks and large two-color blocks together. Referring to placement diagram, stitch brown triangles and small blocks to afghan for pumpkin stems. Stitch large triangles to afghan for bats. For face on top pumpkin, stitch 2 small triangles for eyes, 1 large triangle for nose, and 5 small blocks and 2 small triangles for mouth. For face on middle pumpkin, stitch 2 small blocks for eyes, 1 large triangle for nose, and 4 small triangles for mouth. For face on bottom pumpkin, stitch 2 small blocks for eyes, 1 large triangle for nose, and 2 large triangles and 2 small blocks for mouth.

Luck of the Irish

Bring a bit of Irish luck into your home with this mile-a-minute variation afghan.

FINISHED SIZE
Approximately 60" square.

MATERIALS
Sportweight acrylic (175-yd. ball): 12 cream, 6 green.
Size F crochet hook, or size to obtain gauge.

GAUGE
10 dc and 6 rows = 2½".

DIRECTIONS
Star block (make 9): *Note:* Carry color not in use around by working over it. With green, ch 4, join with a sl st to form a ring. **Rnd 1:** Ch 3 for first dc, 2 dc in ring, (ch 3, 3 dc in ring) 3 times, ch 3, sl st in top of beg ch-3.

   Rnd 2: Ch 3 for first dc, dc in ea of next 2 dc, * ch 1, (3 dc, ch 3, 3 dc) in ch-3 sp for corner, ch 1, dc in ea of next 3 dc, rep from * around, end with sl st in top of beg ch-3.

   Rnd 3: Sl st backward into ch-1 sp, ch 3 for first dc, dc in same sp, drop green and carry it across by working over it, join cream, dc in same sp, * dc in next ch-1 sp, drop cream and carry it across by working over it, using green, 2 dc in same ch-1 sp, 2 dc in corner sp, drop green, using cream, (dc, ch 3, dc) in same corner sp, drop cream, using green, 2 dc in same corner sp **, 2 dc in next ch-1 sp, drop green, using cream, dc in same ch-1 sp, rep from * around, ending last rep at **, sl st in top of beg ch-3.

   Rnd 4: Sl st backward into dc just made, ch 3 for first dc, dc in next st, * drop green, using cream, dc in ea of next 4 sts, drop cream, using green, keeping last lp of ea st on hook, dc in ea of next 2 sts, yo and pull through all lps on hook (dc dec over 2 sts made), drop green, using cream, dc in ea of next 2 sts, (3 dc, ch 3, 3 dc) in corner ch-3 sp, dc in ea of next 2 sts, drop cream, using green, dc dec over next 2 sts, rep from * around, end with sl st in top of beg ch-3. Fasten off cream.

   Rnd 5: With green, working in ft lps only, * sc in ea st to corner, sc in ea ch of corner ch-3 sp, rep from * around. Fasten off.

Square with green corner (make 16): With cream, ch 4, join with a sl st to form a ring. **Rnd 1:** Ch 3 for first dc, 2 dc in ring, (ch 3, 3 dc in ring) 3 times, ch 3, sl st in top of beg ch-3.

Rnd 2: Ch 3 for first dc, dc in ea of next 2 dc, ch 1, * (2 dc, ch 3, 2 dc) in ch-3 sp for corner, ch 1, dc in ea of next 3 dc, ch 1, rep from * around, end with sl st in top of beg ch-3.

Rnd 3: Sl st backward into ch-1 sp, ch 3 for first dc, 2 dc in same sp, 3 dc in next ch-1 sp, * (2 dc, ch 3, 2 dc) in corner ch-3 sp, (3 dc in next ch-1 sp) twice, rep from * around, end with sl st in top of beg ch-3.

Rnd 4: Ch 3 for first dc, dc in ea of next 2 sts, ch 1, (dc in ea of next 3 sts), * ch 1, dc in ea of next 2 sts, ch 1, (2 dc, ch 3, 2 dc) in corner ch-3 sp, ch 1, dc in ea of next 2 sts, (ch 1, dc in ea of next 3 sts) twice, rep from * once more, ch 1, dc in ea of next 2 sts, ch 1, dc in corner ch-3 sp, join green, drop cream and carry it across by working over it, (dc, ch 3, dc) in corner, drop green, do not carry across, using cream, dc in same corner sp, ch 1, dc in ea of next 2 sts, (ch 1, dc in ea of next 3 sts) twice, ch 1, dc in ea of next 2 sts, ch 1, (2 dc, ch 3, 2 dc) in corner ch-3 sp, ch 1, dc in ea of next 2 sts, ch 1, sl st in top of beg ch-3.

Rnd 5: Sl st backward into ch-1 sp, ch 3 for first dc, 2 dc in same sp, 3 dc in ea of next 3 ch-1 sps, * (3 dc, ch 3, 3 dc) in corner sp, 3 dc in ea of next 5 ch-1 sps, rep from * once more, drop cream and carry it across, using green, (3 dc, ch 3, 3 dc) in corner sp, fasten off green, using cream, 3 dc in ea of next 5 ch-1 sps, (3 dc, ch 3, 3 dc) in corner sp, 3 dc in next ch-1 sp, sl st in top of beg ch-3. Fasten off.

Solid block (make 48 cream): **Row 1:** Ch 22, dc in 4th ch from hook and ea ch across, turn = 20 sts.

Rows 2–11: Ch 3 for first dc, dc in ea st across, turn. Fasten off after row 11.

Quarter-circle block (make 36): **Row 1:** With green, ch 4, 2 dc in 4th ch from hook, turn.

Row 2: Ch 3 for first dc, dc in same st, 3 dc in next st, 2 dc in last st, turn.

Row 3: Ch 3 for first dc, 2 dc in next st, dc in ea of next 3 sts, 2 dc in next st, dc in last st, turn.

Row 4: Ch 3 for first dc, 2 dc in next st, dc in ea of next 5 sts, 2 dc in next st, dc in last st, turn.

Row 5: Ch 3 for first dc, dc in same st, dc in ea of next 3 sts, 2 dc in next st, dc in next st, 2 dc in next st, dc in ea of next 3 sts, 2 dc in last st, turn.

Row 6: Ch 3 for first dc, dc in ea of next 2 sts, 2 dc in next st, (dc in ea of next 3 sts, 2 dc in next st) twice, dc in ea of last 3 sts, turn.

Row 7: Ch 3 for first dc, dc in same st, dc in ea of next 6 sts, 2 dc in next st, dc in next st, 2 dc in next st, dc in ea of next 7 sts, 2 dc in last st, turn.

Row 8: Ch 3 for first dc, dc in ea of next 4 sts, 2 dc in next st, dc in ea of next 10 sts, 2 dc in next st, dc in ea of next 5 sts, turn.

Row 9: Ch 3 for first dc, dc in same st, dc in ea of next 8 sts, 2 dc in next st, dc in ea of next 3 sts, 2 dc in next st, dc in ea of next 10 sts, turn.

Row 10: Ch 1, sc in same st, sc in ea of next 4 sts, hdc in ea of next 2 sts, (dc in ea of next 2 sts, 2 dc in next st) 3 times, dc in ea of next 2 sts, hdc in ea of next 2 sts, sc in ea of last 7 sts, turn. Fasten off.

Row 11: Join cream with sl st in last sc of row 10, sc in same st, sc in ea of next 4 sts, hdc in ea of next 4 sts, dc in ea of next 5 sts, 2 tr in next st, 3 dtr in next st for corner, 2 tr in next st, dc in ea of next 5 sts, hdc in ea of next 4 sts, sc in ea of last 5 sts, turn.

Row 12: Ch 1, sc in same st and ea of next 3 sts, hdc in ea of next 5 sts, dc in ea of next 5 sts, tr in ea of next 2 sts, 2 dtr in next st, 3 dtr in next st, 2 dtr in next st, tr in ea of next 2 sts, dc in ea of next 5 sts, hdc in ea of next 5 sts, sc in ea of last 4 sts, turn.

Row 13: Ch 1, sc in same st and ea of next 16 sts, hdc in ea of next 2 sts, (2 dc, ch 1, 2 dc) in next st for corner, hdc in ea of next 2 sts, sc in ea of last 17 sts across. Fasten off.

Short strip (make 12): With green, ch 6, join with a sl st to form a ring. **Row 1** (right side): Ch 4 for first tr, (3 tr, ch 3, 4 tr) in ring, turn.

Rows 2 and 3: Ch 4, (4 tr, ch 3, 4 tr) in ch-3 sp bet shells, turn. Fasten off after row 3.

Border: Row 1: With right side facing, join cream with sl st in beg ch-6 ring, ch 4 for first tr, 2 tr in ring, working across side of center section, 4 dc bet next 2 shells, 4 dc in next ch-4 sp, 15 tr in ch-3 sp bet shells at end of center section, working across opposite side of center section, 4 dc bet next 2 shells, 4 dc in next ch-4 sp, 3 tr in beg ring, turn.

Row 2: Ch 3 for first dc, dc in ea of next 14 sts, (2 dc, ch 3, 2 dc) in next st for corner, dc in ea of next 5 sts, (2 dc, ch 3, 2 dc) in next st for corner, dc in ea of next 15 sts, turn.

Row 3: Ch 3 for first dc, dc in ea of next 16 sts, (2 dc, ch 3, 2 dc) in next ch-3 sp, dc in ea of next 9 sts, (2 dc, ch 3, 2 dc) in next ch-3 sp, dc in ea of next 17 sts, turn.

Row 4: Ch 1, sc in same st, [sc in ea st to corner sp, (sc, ch 1, sc) in corner ch-3 sp] twice, sc in ea rem st. Fasten off.

Long strip (make 12): With green, ch 6, join with a sl st to form a ring. **Row 1** (right side): Ch 4 for first tr, (3 tr, ch 3, 4 tr) in ring, turn.

Rows 2–16: Rep row 2 as for short strip. Fasten off after row 16.

Border: Rnd 1: With right side facing, join cream with sl st in beg ring, ch 4 for first tr, 14 tr in same ring, working across side of center section, (4 dc bet next 2 shells, 4 dc in next ch-4 sp) across to end of center section, 15 tr in ch-3 sp bet 2 shells at end of center section, working across opposite side of center section, (4 dc in next ch-4 sp, 4 dc bet next 2 shells) across, end with sl st in top of beg ch-4.

Rnd 2: Ch 3 for first dc, dc in ea of next 3 tr, * (2 dc, ch 3, 2 dc) in next tr for corner, dc in ea of next 5 tr, (2 dc, ch 3, 2 dc) in next tr for corner, dc in ea of next 4 tr, dc in ea dc across **, dc in ea of next 4 tr, rep from * to ** once more, sl st in top of beg ch-3.

Rnd 3: Ch 3 for first dc, * dc in ea st to corner sp, (2 dc, ch 3, 2 dc) in corner ch-3 sp, rep from * around, sl st in top of beg ch-3.

Rnd 4: Ch 1, sc in same st, * sc in ea st to corner sp, (sc, ch 1, sc) in corner ch-3 sp, rep from * around, sl st in first sc. Fasten off.

Assembly: With right sides facing and referring to placement diagram, whipstitch pieces together. Work in back loops only to join star blocks.

Edging: Join cream with sl st in any corner sp, ch 3 for first dc, dc in same sp, * [dc in ea st to 1 st before joining, keeping last lp of ea st on hook, dc in last st of same piece and first st of next piece, yo and pull through all lps on hook (dc dec made over joining)] across to next corner sp, (2 dc, ch 1, 2 dc) in corner sp, rep from * around, end with sl st in top of beg ch-3.

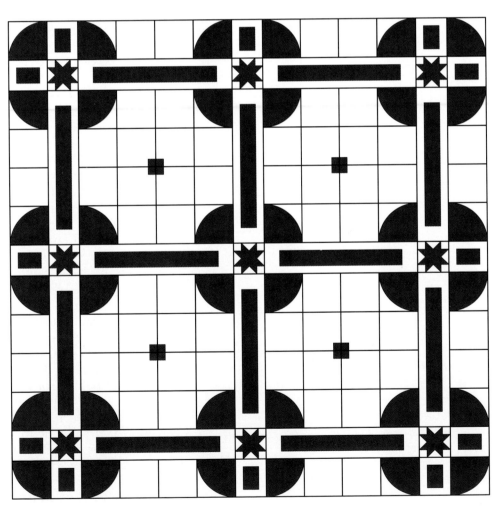

Placement Diagram

General Directions

CROCHET ABBREVIATIONS

beg	begin(ning)
bet	between
bk lp(s)	back loop(s)
ch	chain(s)
ch-	refers to chain previously made
cl	cluster(s)
cont	continu(e) (ing)
dc	double crochet
dec	decrease(s) (d) (ing)
dtr	double triple crochet
ea	each
est	established
foll	follow(s) (ing)
ft lp(s)	front loop(s)
grp(s)	group(s)
hdc	half double crochet
inc	increase(s) (d) (ing)
lp(s)	loop(s)
pat(s)	pattern(s)
prev	previous
rem	remain(s) (ing)
rep	repeat(s)
rnd(s)	round(s)
sc	single crochet
sk	skip(ped)
sl st	slip stitch
sp(s)	space(s)
st(s)	stitch(es)
tch	turning chain
tog	together
tr	triple crochet
yo	yarn over

Repeat whatever follows * as indicated. "Rep from * 3 times more" means to work 4 times in all.

Work directions given in parentheses and brackets the number of times specified or in the place specified.

GAUGE

Before beginning a project, work a 4"-square gauge swatch using the recommended-size hook. Count and compare the number of stitches per inch in the swatch with the designer's gauge. If you have fewer stitches in your swatch, try a smaller hook; if you have more stitches, try a larger hook.

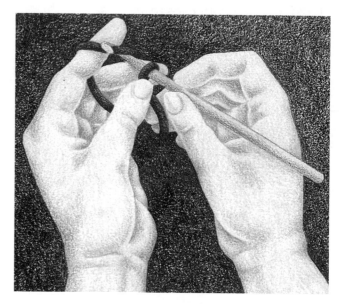

WORKING TOGETHER

Hold the hook as you would a pencil (shown here) or a piece of chalk. Weave the yarn through the fingers of your left hand to control the amount of yarn fed into the work and to provide tension. Once work has begun, the thumb and middle finger of the left hand come into play, pressing together to hold the stitches just made.

SLIP STITCH DIAGRAM

Here a slip stitch (sl st) is used to join a ring. Taking care not to twist ch, insert hook into first ch, yo and pull through ch and lp on hook (sl st made). The sl st can also be used to join finished pieces (see page 141) or to move across a group of sts without adding height to the work.

SLIP KNOT DIAGRAM
Loop the yarn around and let the loose end of the yarn fall behind the loop to form a pretzel shape as shown. Insert the hook (**A**) and pull both ends to close the knot (**B**).

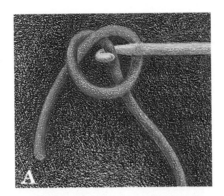

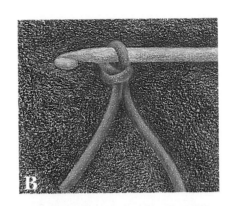

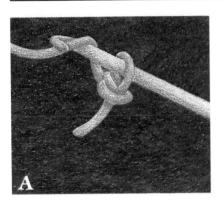

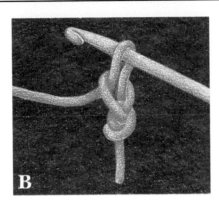

CHAIN STITCH DIAGRAM
A. Place a slip knot on your hook. With hands in the position shown above, and with the thumb and middle finger of the left hand holding the yarn end, wrap the yarn up and over the hook (from back to front). This movement is called a "yarn over (yo)" and is basic to every crochet stitch.

B. Use the hook to pull the yarn through the loop (lp) already on the hook. The combination of yo and pulling the yarn through the lp makes 1 chain stitch (ch.)

C. Repeat until the ch is the desired length, trying to keep the movements even and relaxed, and all the ch stitches (sts) the same size. Hold the ch near the working area to keep it from twisting. Count sts as shown in diagram. (Do not count lp on hook or slip knot.)

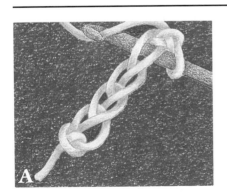

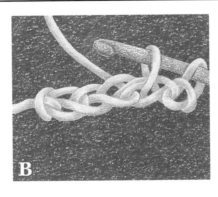

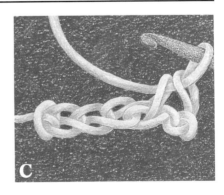

SINGLE CROCHET DIAGRAM
A. Insert hook under top 2 lps of 2nd ch from hook and yo. (Always work sts through top 2 lps unless directions specify otherwise.)

B. Pull yarn through ch (2 lps on hook).

C. Yo and pull yarn through 2 lps on hook (1 sc made.)

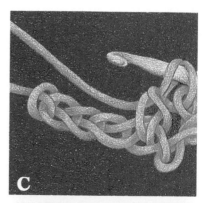

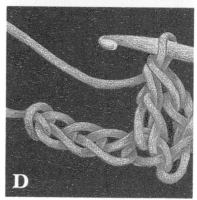

DOUBLE CROCHET DIAGRAM

A. Yo, insert hook into 4th ch from hook, and yo.

B. Pull yarn through ch (3 lps on hook).

C. Yo and pull through 2 lps on hook (2 lps remaining). (*Note:* When directions say

"keeping last lp of ea st on hook," this means to work the specified st to the final yo. This is done to make a cluster or to work a decrease.)

D. Yo and pull through 2 remaining (rem) lps (1 dc made).

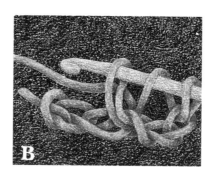

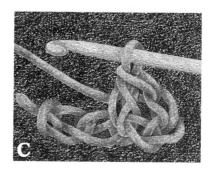

HALF DOUBLE CROCHET DIAGRAM

A. Yo and insert hook into 3rd ch from hook.

B. Yo and pull through ch (3 lps on hook).

C. Yo and pull yarn through all 3 lps on hook (1 hdc made).

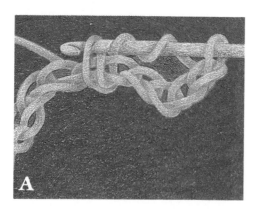

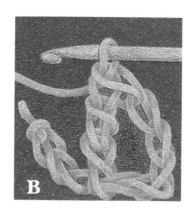

TRIPLE CROCHET DIAGRAM

A. Yo twice, insert hook into 5th ch from hook. Yo and pull through ch (4 lps on hook).

B. Yo and pull through 2 lps on hook (3 lps rem). Yo and pull through 2 lps on hook (2 lps rem). Yo and pull through 2 lps on hook (1 tr made).

140

ASSEMBLY

To assemble crocheted pieces when making an afghan, use a yarn needle to whipstitch (**A**) or a crochet hook to slip stitch (**B**) the pieces together. Pieces can also be joined using single crochet stitches, but this makes a heavier seam.

When making squares or other pieces to be stitched together, leave a 20" tail of yarn when fastening off. This yarn tail can then be used to stitch the pieces together. Also, be sure all stitches and rows of the squares or strips are aligned and running in the same direction.

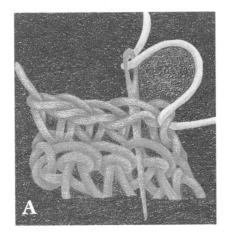

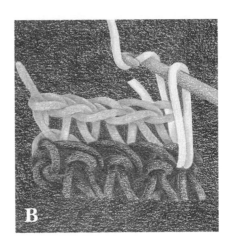

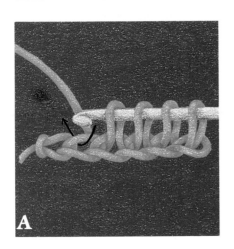

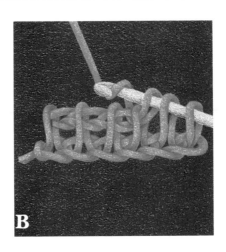

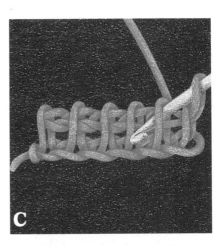

AFGHAN STITCH DIAGRAM

A. *Row 1: Step 1:* Keeping all lps on hook, pull up a lp through top lp only, in 2nd ch from hook and each ch across = same number of lps and ch. Do not turn.

B. *Step 2:* Yo and pull through first lp on hook, * yo and pull through 2 lps on hook, rep from * across (1 lp rem on hook for first lp of next row). Do not turn.

C. *Row 2: Step 1:* Keeping all lps on hook, pull up a lp from under 2nd vertical bar, * pull up a lp from under next vertical bar, rep from * across. Do not turn. *Step 2:* Rep step 2 of row 1.

Rep both steps of row 2 for the required number of rows. Fasten off after last row by working a sl st in each bar across.

D. When the fabric is finished, it is a perfect grid for cross-stitch.

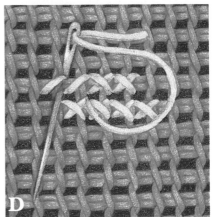

Yarn Information

The following is a complete list of the yarns used for each project pictured in the book. Visit your local yarn shop to obtain the yarn shown or for help in substituting another yarn. If you are unable to locate the yarn in your area or for further information, write the yarn company at the address listed on page 144.

Mosaic Medallions, page 8, Brunswick Yarns, Pearl (50-gr., 110-yd. skein): 31 White #5900.

Nursery Rhymes, page 10, Plymouth Yarn Company, Cleo (50-gr., 109-yd. ball): 3 each White #384, Light Yellow #372; 4 each Baby Pink #391, Mint Green #418, Baby Blue #392, Aqua #401, Purple #394.

Ruffled Yo-Yos, page 12, DMC Corporation, Brilliant Knitting/Crochet Cotton (218-yd. ball): 17 White; 1 each Nile Green #954, Light Rose #3326, Medium Lavender #210.

Buttoned-Down, page 14, Georges Picaud, Rocaille (50-gr., 66-yd. skein): 5 Variegated Mauve/Green/Ecru #2. Filatura Di Crosa, Sympathie (50-gr., 146-yd. skein): 5 Dark Rose #963, 1 Turquoise #709.

Count to Nine, page 16, Plymouth Yarn Company, Cleo Plus (50-gr., 106-yd. ball): 2 Medium Country Blue #1025; 4 each Light Country Green #1021, Medium Country Green #1567, 4 Medium Aqua #1019; 9 Medium Country Purple #1018.

Teatime, page 18, Brunswick Yarns, Fore-'n-Aft Sport (50-gr., 175-yd. ball): 15 White #6000.

Bright Blossoms, page 22, Brunswick Yarns, Fore-'n-Aft Sport (50-gr., 175-yd. ball): 1 each Maize #60031, Poppy Red #6022; 2 each Extra Hot Pink #6098, Deep Blue Velvet #6081; 3 Saffron #6008; 4 Cardinal #6024; 6 Holly Green #60043. Pingouin, Pingofrance (50-gr., 150-yd. ball): 2 Plum #123.

Checkmate, page 24, Brunswick Yarns, Fore-'n-Aft Sport (50-gr., 175-yd. ball): 4 White #6000, 8 Cardinal #6024.

Plain Geometry, page 26, Pingouin, Pingofrance (50-gr., 150-yd. ball): 2 Green #176. Brunswick Yarns, Fore-'n-Aft Sport (50-gr., 175-yd. ball): 3 Saffron #6008; 2 each Blue Blaze #6042, Extra Hot Pink #6098; 1 Scarlet #6021.

Pyramids, page 28, Brunswick Yarns, Pearl (50-gr., 110-yd. skein): 4 each Willow #5920, Dusty Pink #5922, Silver Gray #5915; 6 Eggshell #59100; 11 Smoke Blue #5921.

Pastel Blanket, page 31, Classic Elite Yarns, Newport (50-gr., 70-yd. skein): 18 Ice #2391, 23 Baby Blue #2329; Newport Light (50-gr., 93-yd. skein): 15 Metallic Blue #3383, 17 Polished Green #3315.

Iris Garden, page 34, Filatura Di Crosa, Stella (50-gr., 138-yd. skein): 7 Light Country Blue #421, 11 Light Taupe #443, 18 Light Country Green #416.

Terrific Ts, page 36, Aarlan, Fleurette (50-gr., 120-yd. ball): 5 Light Peach #4473, 10 Variegated Cream/Peach/Blue #2631, 13 Pale Blue #4474.

Blue & White Nine-patch, page 38, Plymouth Yarn Company, Cleo (50-gr., 109-yd. ball): 13 White #384, 16 Baby Blue #392.

Poppies, page 40, Filatura Di Crosa, Sympathie (50-gr., 146-yd. skein): 2 Light Country Green #955, 3 Dark Rose #963, 4 Yellow #909, 5 Medium Rose #964, 14 Light Rose #946.

Grandmother's Flowers, page 44, Plymouth Yarn Company, Cleo (50-gr., 109-yd. ball): 10 Cream #525; 9 Dark Green #567; 8 Light Rose #441; 4 Dark Rose #538; 3 each Mint Green #418, Blue #399; 2 Dark Purple #439; 1 Burgundy #532.

Wild Goose Chase, page 46, Plymouth Yarn Company, Cleo (50-gr., 109-yd. ball): 2 each Gray #404, Aqua #401; 3 each Mint Green #418, Light Yellow #372, Baby Pink #391. Aarlan, Fleurette (50-gr., 120-yd. ball): 2 each Light Green #4493, Tan #4490, Light Blue #4462; Fleurette Mouline (50-gr., 120-yd. ball): 10 Variegated Aqua/Blue/Pink #2632.

Log Cabin Blues, page 48, Brunswick Yarns, Fore-'n-Aft Sport (50-gr., 175-yd. ball): 14 Ecru #60000, 15 Deep Blue Velvet #6081, 16 Medium Blue Velvet #60812.

Old-fashioned Fans, page 50, Filatura Di Crosa, Sympathie (50-gr., 146-yd. skein): 13 Medium Rose #964. Little Wool Company, Imported Specialty Yarn (200-gr., 900-yd. skein): 1 Tourmaline.

Oh My Stars, page 52, Brunswick Yarns, Pearl Sport (50-gr., 165-yd. ball): 3 each Cream #49100, Peach

#4919, Cool Mint #4923, Dusty Pink #4922; 6 Jade #4934.

Little Red Schoolhouse, page 54, Plymouth Yarn Company, Cleo (50-gr., 109-yd. ball): 10 each Brown #376, Light Brown #378; 5 Natural #383; 3 Rust #407; 2 Scarlet #375; 1 Gold #381.

Honeycomb, page 57, Plymouth Yarn Company, Cleo (50-gr., 109-yd. ball): 10 each Dark Aqua #019, Light Yellow #372; 7 White #384; 6 each Medium Aqua #021, Light Rose #371, Dark Rose #409; 3 Medium Country Purple #018.

Basketweave, page 60, Brunswick Yarns, Pearl Sport (50-gr., 165-yd. ball): 4 Peach #4919; 5 each Dusty Pink #4922, Cool Mint #4923; 6 Cream #49100.

Trip Around the World, page 62, Reynolds Yarns, Reynelle Deluxe (100-gr., 240-yd. skein): 1 Light Purple #8009; 2 each Blue #8084, Light Rose #8091; 3 Dark Purple #8008; 7 Medium Rose #8092.

Prairie Memories, page 64, Filatura Di Crosa, Sympathie (50-gr., 146-yd. skein): 20 Earth Brown #753.

Country Tweed, page 66, Plymouth Yarn Company, Cleo Plus (50-gr., 106-yd. ball): 13 Very Light Taupe #1500; 6 each Medium Taupe #1011, Light Tangerine #1003; 5 each Terra Cotta #1001, Medium Country Purple #1018, Light Country Green #1021; 4 Medium Aqua #1019; 3 each Medium Country Blue #1025, Medium Country Green #1567.

Checkered Throw, page 68, Filatura Di Crosa, Sympathie (50-gr., 146-yd. skein): 5 Peach #910, 12 Light Country Green #955.

Irish Chain, page 70, Plymouth Yarn Company, Cleo (50-gr., 109-yd. ball): 5 Purple #394. Aarlan, Fleurette (50-gr., 120-yd. ball): 16 Light Blue #4462.

Tumbling Blocks, page 72, Reynolds Yarns, Reynelle Deluxe (100-gr., 240-yd. skein): 2 Cream #8079; 4 each Light Gray #8069, Medium Gray #8064, Dark Gray #8062.

White Lace Coverlet, page 74, Brunswick Yarns, Moon Beams (50-gr., 100-yd. skein): 13 White #8500. DMC Corporation, Brilliant Knitting/Crochet Cotton (218-yd. ball): 2 White.

Simple Pieces, page 78, Filatura Di Crosa, Sympathie (50-gr., 146-yd. skein): 3 each Peach #910, Yellow #909; 4 Light Country Green #955, 15 Light Country Blue #940.

Warm 'n Woolly, page 80, Brunswick Yarns, Sheepswool (100-gr., 260-yd. skein): 1 each Light Oriental Rose #3158, Rich Teal #31271, Light Willow #3157, Dark Colonial Blue #31183; 2 each Oriental Rose #31581, Medium Oriental Rose #31582, Dark Oriental Rose #31583, Light Rich Teal #3127, Medium Rich Teal #31273, Dark Rich Teal #31274, Willow #31571, Medium Willow #31572, Dark Willow #31573, Light Colonial Blue #3118, Colonial Blue #31181, Medium Colonial Blue #31182.

Fair Play, page 82, Brunswick Yarns, Fore-'n-Aft Sport (50-gr., 175-yd. ball): 4 Cardinal #6024; 2 each Dark Green #6044, Navy #6016, Irish Green #6049, Deep Hyacinth #6099; 1 Saffron #6008.

Amish Stripes, page 84, Filatura Di Crosa, 501 (50-gr., 137-yd. skein): 12 Black #115, 6 Dark Purple #113, 3 Medium Aqua #110; Sympathie (50-gr., 146-yd. skein): 4 Dark Rose #912.

A-"Maze" Yourself, page 87, Plymouth Yarn Company, Cleo (50-gr., 109-yd. ball): 8 Natural #383; 5 Light Brown #378; 4 each Terra Cotta #001, Green #406, Brown #376.

Whirling Pinwheels, page 90, Filatura Di Crosa, Stella (50-gr., 138-yd. skein): 9 Cream #434, 8 Teal #438.

Jewel Diamonds, page 92, Brunswick Yarns, Fore-'n-Aft Sport (50-gr., 175-yd. ball): 9 Maroon #6026, 5 Dark Green #6044, 3 Navy #6016. Reynolds Yarns, Reynelle Deluxe (100-gr. 240-yd. skein): 5 Navy #8011.

Playful Diamonds, page 94, Reynolds Yarns, Reynelle Deluxe (100-gr., 240-yd. skein): 2 Orange #8033, 3 Periwinkle Blue #8075, 4 Rose #8072. Brunswick Yarns, Fore-'n-Aft Sport (50-gr., 175-yd. ball): 12 Ecru #60000.

Forest of Pines, page 96, Brunswick Yarns, Regal Sport (50-gr., 175-yd. ball): 1 Indigo #4610; Fore-'n-Aft Sport (50-gr., 175-yd. ball): 3 each Dark Green #6044, Mocha Heather #6029; 18 Fisherman #60300.

Kaleidoscope, page 98, Plymouth Yarn Company, Cleo (50-gr., 109-yd. ball): 3 Rust #407; 4 each Gold #381, Brown #376, Light Brown #378, Green #406; 7 Natural #383.

Special Effects, page 100, Filatura Di Crosa, Alpaca Peru (50-gr., 199-yd. skein): 11 Natural #20; 8 each Medium Earth Brown #60, Dark Earth Brown #30; 4 Medium Country Blue #29.

Fancy Fencing, page 102, Reynolds Yarns, Reynelle Deluxe (100-gr., 240-yd. skein): 3 each Cream #8079,

Blue #8084; 4 Medium Rose #8092; 5 Dark Rose #8071.

Fade to Black, page 104, Reynolds Yarns, Reynelle Deluxe (100-gr., 240-yd. skein): 3 each Dark Gray #8062, Medium Gray #8064; 5 Light Gray #8069.

Classic Patchwork, page 106, Classic Elite Yarns, Newport (50-gr., 70-yd. skein): 9 Meadow Green #2321; 7 each Oyster #2386, Natural #2316; 6 Ashes of Rose #2340; 5 Canyon #2306; 3 each Pebble #2345, Wiscasset Brick #2342, Toffee #2344; 2 each Honey Mustard #2341, Winterport #2352, Indigo Blue #2305; 1 each Olive #2339, Baby Blue #2329, Sterling #2323, Faded Blue #2308, Terra Cotta #2343, Peach Melba #2363.

Red, White & True, page 110, Brunswick Yarns, Regal Sport (50-gr., 175-yd. ball): 5 each Indigo #4610, Holiday Red #4620; 6 White #4600.

For My Valentine, page 112, Reynolds Yarns, Reynelle Deluxe (100-gr., 240-yd. skein): 2 Medium Rose #8092, 3 Light Rose #8091, 4 Rose #8072, 12 Cream #8079.

Spring Rainbow, page 115, Reynolds Yarns, Reynelle Deluxe (100-gr., 240-yd. skein): 6 Baby Blue #8019; 2 each Light Purple #8009, Aqua #8077; 1 each Light Yellow #8038, Peach #8074, Baby Pink #8048, Mint Green #8028.

Nutcracker Sweet, page 116, Plymouth Yarn Company, Cleo (50-gr., 109-yd. ball): 4 each Light Yellow #372, Baby Pink #391, Mint Green #418, Aqua #401; 5 White #384, 7 Purple #394, 11 Baby Blue #392. DMC Corporation, Size 5 Perle Cotton (27-yd. skein): 2 each Very Light Peach #948, Medium Pink #776, Dark Golden Brown #975, Pearl Gray #415; 1 each Light Baby Blue #3325, Dark Steel Gray #414, Tan #436, Light Pale Yellow #745.

Christmas Wishes, page 120, Pinguoin, Le Yarn 3 (100-gr., 200-yd. skein): 18 Beige Heather #406. Brunswick Yarns, Fore-'n-Aft Sport (50-gr., 175-yd. ball): 1 Holly Green #60043; Pearl (50-gr., 110-yd. skein): 1 Burgundy #5924.

Snowflakes, page 124, Filatura Di Crosa, Diwa (50-gr., 202-yd. skein): 7 Light Blue #27, 9 Cream #9.

Autumn Flight, page 126, Classic Elite Yarns, Newport Light (50-gr., 93-yd. skein): 6 Gold #3381; 7 each Rust #3351, Brown #3330; 27 Natural #3316.

Deck the Halls, page 128, Brunswick Yarns, Fore-'n-Aft Sport (50-gr., 175-yd. ball): 15 Ecru #60000, 4 Irish Green #6049, 1 Mocha Heather #6029. DMC Corporation, Size 5 Perle Cotton (27-yd. skein): 1 each Light Violet #554, Medium Garnet #815, Dark Antique Blue #930, Light Coral #352, Very Dark Lavender #208, Ecru.

Slices of Summer, page 130, Brunswick Yarns, Fore-'n-Aft Sport (50-gr., 175-yd. ball): 5 Holly Green #60043, 6 Cardinal #6024, 11 White #6000.

Pumpkin Trio, page 132, Filatura Di Crosa, Stella (50-gr., 138-yd. skein): 1 each Dark Country Blue #422, Brown #436; 3 Dark Country Green #433; 8 Medium Country Green #432. Emu, Superwash DK (50-gr., 123-yd. ball): 2 Medium Orange #3014, 6 Light Orange #3015. Brunswick Yarns, Sheepswool (100-gr., 260-yd. skein): 3 Colonial Blue #31181. Filatura Di Crosa, 501 (50-gr., 137-yd. skein): 1 Black #115.

Luck of the Irish, page 134, Brunswick Yarns, Fore-'n-Aft Sport (50-gr., 175-yd. ball): 12 Ecru #60000, 6 Holly Green #60043.

Yarn Companies

Brunswick Yarns
P.O. Box 276
Pickens, SC 29671

Classic Elite Yarns
12 Perkins Street
Lowell, MA 01854

DMC Corporation
10 Port Kearney
South Kearney, NJ 07032

Emu/Robin Yarns
c/o Plymouth Yarn
    Company
500 Lafayette Street
Bristol, PA 19007

Filatura Di Crosa
c/o Stacy Charles
    Collection
119 Green Street
Brooklyn, NY 11222

Pingouin
c/o Laninter Corp.
P.O. Box 1542
Mount Pleasant,
    SC 29465

Plymouth Yarn
    Company, Inc.
P.O. Box 28
Bristol, PA 19007

Reynolds Yarns
A division of JCA, Inc.
35 Scales Lane
Townsend, MA
    01469-1094